Caroline

WHO AM I?

DISCUSSION SERIES: 12

Who am I?

identity, adoption and
human fertilisation

◆

*Christine Walby
& Barbara Symons*

BRITISH AGENCIES FOR
ADOPTION & FOSTERING

PUBLISHED BY
BRITISH AGENCIES FOR
ADOPTION & FOSTERING
11 SOUTHWARK STREET
LONDON SE1 1RQ
© BAAF 1990
ISBN 0 903534 87 8
ISSN 0260 082 X
DESIGNED BY ANDREW HAIG
TYPESET BY ETHNOGRAPHICA LTD
PRINTED AND BOUND IN ENGLAND

The views expressed in this publication are those of the authors and not necessarily those of British Agencies for Adoption & Fostering.

Contents

Acknowledgements

This book is essentially about people and many have contributed, directly and indirectly, to its writing. John Gamble OBE, the former Director of Social Services, and other colleagues in South Glamorgan who facilitated the original research; Dr Ron Walton of Cardiff University who provided tutorial guidance and support; the various typists who helped with the transcribing of tapes and preparation of the manuscript – all these deserve mention and thanks.

At the stage of establishing the discussion group when we were trying to put individual perceptions and experiences into a collective context, the positive and practical assistance provided by the Mental Health Foundation was especially appreciated. Their grant did more than finance the early group meetings, it gave us heart to continue.

Some of the people who have contributed to the book have not been personally known to us. They have heard of what we have been doing and have made contact in order to express interest, satisfaction and, sometimes, relief that important issues which have concerned them and their families have been identified and brought into the open. In this anonymous but nonetheless sincere way, we wish to express our gratitude for these contacts.

Our particular and warmest thanks must be reserved, however, for those who participated in the study, especially those who formed the membership of the on-going group. It was our pleasure and privilege to share some very important experiences – some happy, some sad, some funny, but always very real.

Establishing families and having children is, for those who choose to do so, a fulfilling and satisfying experience, however the children come into the family. We hope that this book will be helpful in encouraging a full consideration and discussion of some of the questions which derive from the particular circumstances of assisted family-building, whether this occurs as a result of adoption or of the reproductive technologies. We share the view, frequently expressed by those whose experiences have shaped this book, that there is little to fear when the truth is presented with confidence and love.

Finally, to the publishing and editorial staff of BAAF, our special thanks for the invaluable help they provided in the preparation of the material for publication.

Christine Walby   Barbara Symons

Introduction

In 1975 a change in the law in England and Wales made it possible for adults over the age of 18 who had been adopted to obtain certain information about their adoption and their original birth registration.[1] Many took advantage of this new facility.

In 1987 a white paper on human fertilisation and embryology was published,[2] following the Warnock Committee of Inquiry on the same subject.[3]

There is perhaps no obvious connection between these two events. However, in this book we will argue that there are key comparisons between the experiences of adopted people and of people conceived through a human fertilisation programme. It follows that we also contend that the professional experience of adoption, stretching over some 60 years since the Adoption of Children Act of 1926, should inform and influence the debate about some of the proposals in the recent white paper. In particular, we shall discuss the proposals about the *right to information* of people born as a result of sperm or embryo donation, where the child is conceived with the intention of separation from one or both of the biological parents.

The white paper makes only passing reference to the important issue of whether potential parents should go through any assessment or selection procedure before gaining access to medical programmes. Again it would seem useful to consider relevant lessons from adoption practice and experience. There are confusions, conflicts and, in our view, omissions in the white paper on a number of major issues on which there is already substantial information. For example, limited appreciation is indicated of the significance of a clear sense of identity in the development of healthy emotional and social maturity. Similarly, the real contribution that adoption research and experience can make to informed and enlightened legislation of human fertilisation and embryology is not acknowledged. These are compelling reasons for urging a thorough debate before, rather than after, introducing legislation.

Indeed, uncertainty is expressed in the white paper about the government stance on some of these issues: it admits that attitudes might change, that the situation will be kept under review, and that retroactive measures could be introduced if considered appropriate. This stance shows little consideration for the children, the genetic parents, or the permanent (nurturing) parents of families created 'artificially', all of whom will feel they have rights, needs and obligations as a result of their role in the family. Such an approach is also questionable given the substantial body of relevant knowledge and experience available in this and other countries. Surely the interests of the individuals who are directly affected by human fertilisation programmes in the most profound sense – the children – demand the fullest debate and clarity in legislation now?

What follows is in two distinct parts. The first (chapters 1 to 4) is a description of the development of adoption as a concept, the history of 'access to records' for adopted people and the findings of a small research project undertaken into the experiences and perceptions of a group of adults who sought access to their birth records following the change of legislation in 1975.[4] This section concludes with some discussion of the implications of the research for professional practice in adoption.

The second part (chapters 5 and 6) briefly summarises the background to the white paper and the Warnock Report on which it was based. It is particularly concerned with the implications of both for questions of identity formation and the relevance of personal information about origins. Where appropriate it draws upon research and practice experience of adoption and highlights the areas where lessons might be learned when contemplating other artificial family-building methods. The Human Fertilisation and Embryology Bill was published in late November 1989, too late for detailed discussion in the following chapters. It is however a faithful reproduction of the white paper, particularly in regard to access to information and therefore does not affect our analysis in any way.

We hope that our contribution will inform and stimulate the debate which we feel is essential in any civilised and responsible community about to embark upon the formal regulation of practice in human fertilisation and embryology. To ignore the lessons of 60 years of adoption practice while we learn again some of the same lessons would be difficult to justify to the generations whose needs might be sacrificed in the process.

References

1 Children Act 1975, section 26.

2 Human fertilisation and embryology: a framework for legislation (Cmnd 259) HMSO, 1987.

3 Report of the Committee of Inquiry into human fertilisation and embryology (Warnock Report) (Cmnd 9314) HMSO, 1984.

4 Walby C M 'Adoption: a question of identity' unpublished thesis, 1982.

1 The historical development of adoption

In this country and in this century adoption has been generally assumed to mean the transfer of rights and responsibilities for a child up to his/or her] age of majority from the natural parents to other adults.[1]

This statement from a survey of practice in fostering and adoption sums up adoption as we know it today: an activity essentially based upon a legal transaction, which has profound personal implications for all those involved.

The nurture of a child by adults other than the biological parents is however a human practice which appears to go back at least as far as human records. McWhinnie[2] notes the earliest formal record of adoption as a 'cuneiform tablet dated as early as 2350BC'. Triseliotis[3] too writes of adoption in early history, citing Oedipus and Moses. However, in this country it was not until the first Adoption of Children Act of 1926 that parental rights could be legally and irrevocably transferred from birth parents to substitute parents by means of a court order.

It is not our intention here to reproduce information which has been well documented elsewhere and is not directly relevant to our purpose. Comprehensive and illuminating accounts of early patterns of substitute parenting may be found in the already-mentioned Triseliotis and McWhinnie studies, as well as in Heywood[4] and Ellison.[5] It is relevant, however, to trace the history of adoption since it became legal in 1926, in order to set subsequent discussion into context.

1926–1950: Establishing the legal framework for adoption
The precursors of the Act of 1926 were the Hopkinson Committee[6] which reported in 1921, and the committee chaired by Mr Justice Tomlin[7] which produced three reports in 1925 and 1926. Perhaps the deliberations of both committees are best understood in the social, political and economic context of the early 1920s.

From the dying embers of the nineteenth century emerged the early glimmers of the changing status of children. Significantly, the main impetus for this change, which was as exciting as it was profound, was the declining birth rate and the high infant mortality rate.* Writing in 1973, Heywood[8] said:

> This change in the balance of population set a premium on the life of children which began the emphasis of the public health movement on maternity and child welfare, but this also had repercussions on the care of even the most neglected children.

The infant mortality rate amongst illegitimate children in particular was most disturbing. For example, in 1872[9] of approximately 50,000 children born annually, 30,000 were said to die in their first year. The Select Committee on Protection of Infant Life, 1871, also commented with horror upon the plight of illegitimate children in lying-in establishments and baby-farming houses.

These concerns spawned important social legislation about infant life protection,[10] compulsory notification of births,[11] and the prevention of cruelty to children,[12] all of which are fundamental to our current preventive and protective legislation.

Interwoven with these basic concerns were developments in the Poor Law, the treatment of juvenile delinquency, increasing emotional and psychological understanding of children, and the Great War of 1914–18.

'Boarding out'
Packman[13] writes of boarding out as being 'more than a century old' at the time of the Curtis Inquiry. As a formal activity it can be traced to the seventeenth century when young people under the care of boards of guardians were placed with wet nurses.

The Poor Law (Amendment) Act of 1834 introduced the concept of boarding out in legislation, and from that time clearer criteria emerged regarding the suitability of foster parents.[14] However, it was really from 1870 onwards that both cottage homes and boarding out gained currency in the move to provide more personalised, rather than institutionalised, care for children.

---

*The birth rate fell from 35.5 live births per 1,000 population in 1870–75, to 29.3 live births per 1,000 population in 1896–1900.

The Poor Law authorities began to develop and to experiment with the concept of substitute family care around 1870. This was for the placement of pauper children who were illegitimate, deserted or orphaned.

The major voluntary child care organisations were also active in this field of work.

During this period boarding out was regarded as a permanent arrangement and parental contact was seen as detrimental. It could therefore be claimed that the root of legalised adoption began here, rather than in the other less satisfactory and informal developments based upon arrangements between individuals and baby farming; both of which practices were open to much well-documented abuse.[15] The continued and rapid development of boarding out also seemed to be a result of concern about the phenomenon of institutionalisation of children and their consequent dependence upon the workhouse when they became adults.

The perceived advantages of this boarding-out or quasi-adoption system were described in evidence to a departmental committee appointed in 1894.[16] Essentially the advantages were seen to be home training, the development of character and learning about roles through family examples. Independence and the development of 'personal affections' were also seen as important as on this last point there were very clear indications of the dawning of understanding about the effects of institutionalisation on children.

Indeed its sentiments find an essentially similar, if more astringent, echo in 1973 in a research study on the children in public care who were waiting for substitute families. This study by Rowe and Lambert[17] highlighted the fact that having had depriving experiences in their own families children in care were in great danger of having these experiences intensified. They needed positive compensatory experiences in care and for the vast majority of children these would best be provided within a substitute family group.

There were other significant influences in the late nineteenth and early twentieth centuries. For example, the reformatory and industrial schools also developed the principle of boarding out as a suitable way of meeting the needs of many delinquent children. Concurrently there was a development of formal psychological understanding of children through the work of Freud, Jung, Adler, MacDougall and Piaget. This was preceded by a great shift in the subject matter of children's literature in the second half of the nineteenth century, from the excessively moral to the exploration of fantasy and imagination.

As Heywood has commented, 'the child's nature became truly differentiated from that of adults and respected in its own right'.[18]

The 1914–18 war could be described as a watershed in the development of society's response to the care of children deprived of their own families. The war highlighted certain social problems, particularly those of illegitimate children. Their numbers inevitably increased during the war years, as did the numbers of children who were orphaned, or who had lost one parent. Of even greater concern was the fact that the death rate of illegitimate children in their first year of life was, as in the early 1890s, twice that for legitimate children.*

Concern for unmarried mothers and their families mounted. In 1918 the National Council for the Unmarried Mother and her Child was founded and sought to improve facilities for mothers and children with a view to keeping them together.

At the same time many informal 'adoption' placements were already being arranged, the work being pioneered by voluntary societies: first was the National Children's Home and Orphanage which began making adoption placements in the 1890s. It was however the effects of the war which gave the real impetus to adoption. Publicity about 'war babies' and orphans of soldiers increased and more adoption societies were formed. These were pioneering charitable organisations and their work underlined the problems engendered by unorganised and non-legalised adoption. The child was not legally a member of his or her adoptive family and could not obtain a birth certificate in the name of that family. Such children could be removed from their 'adopters' by birth parents, or birth parents could be called upon to resume responsibility for them.

The early committees of inquiry
These problems stimulated public demand for legal adoption, and a Committee of Inquiry was set up in August 1920 under the chairmanship of Sir Alfred Hopkinson KC. Having reviewed the situation in this country and the provisions made in other countries,

---

*Deaths of infants under one year of age per 1,000 live births in England and Wales: in 1914, 100 legitimate, 207 illegitimate; in 1918, 91 legitimate, 186 illegitimate.

the committee concluded that there was an urgent need for legal provision to be made for adoption in Great Britain. It felt that family life was preferable to institutional life, and that the welfare of the child was of paramount importance. The interests of the child were however seen to be largely compatible with the desire of a childless couple to have children, their need for children being seen as a guarantee for the well-being of the child. However, the committee stressed that initially all efforts should be made to maintain the integrity of the mother/child relationship:

> ... in order to secure the true welfare of the child, all possible encouragement should be given to the efforts of philanthropic persons who seek to avert such severance taking place on economic grounds.[19]

Various bills arising from the report were dropped mainly because of the divergence of views being expressed.[20] This led to the appointment of another committee, chaired by Mr Justice Tomlin.[21]

The Tomlin Committee concluded, with some reservations, that legalised adoption should be introduced. As discussed later, it also expressed concern about the policy of complete secrecy practised by adoption agencies.

The Tomlin Committee produced three reports which led directly to the Adoption of Children Act 1926 and the Adoption of Children (Scotland) Act 1930. These Acts had many similarities and established the main provisions of legal adoption as we know it today. Essentially they created a legal relationship between adopters and adopted children similar to that between birth parents and their children. The main exception was the right to inheritance which continued to derive from the birth parent.

In detail the legislation prescribed criteria for the ages of adopters, giving and dispensing with consents, legalising *de facto* adoptions, and for the establishment of an Adopted Children's Register. A fascinating and significant difference between the two Acts was that in England and Wales machinery was created to enable a traceable connection between entries in the Births Register and the Adopted Children's Register but only to be disclosed on the order of 'a competent jurisdiction',[22] whereas in Scotland information relating the entry in the Adopted Children's Register to the original birth entry could be made directly available to adopted people over 17 years.[23] It took nearly 50 years for the Scottish concept to be extended to England and Wales. We will return to the implementation of that facility.

The Acts also enshrined the principle of basing decisions upon the best interests of the child by placing an obligation upon the court to satisfy itself before making an order that 'it will be for the welfare of the infant, due consideration being for this purpose given to the wishes of the infant having regard to the age and understanding of the infant.' This principle was first highlighted by the Hopkinson Committee in 1921, and was eventually enshrined in the Children Act 1975.* It was further stressed in the interim period, as for example by a committee chaired by Miss Florence Horsburgh MP in 1936:

> It appears to us beyond question that the first duty of the adoption society is to the child.[24]

As the above statement implies, the Horsburgh Committee was set up to inquire into the methods of adoption societies and agencies which by this time were proliferating. The report resulted in the Adoption of Children (Regulation) Act 1939, which legislated for the registration and supervision of adoption societies.[25]

In 1945 an inter-departmental committee was set up 'to inquire into existing methods of providing for children who from loss of parents or from any cause whatever are deprived of a normal home life with their own parents or relatives; and to consider what further measures should be taken to ensure that these children are brought up under conditions best calculated to compensate them for the lack of parent care.' This committee under the chairmanship of Miss Myra Curtis led to one of the most famous milestones in the history of public care for children: the Children Act 1948. Of adoption the Curtis Committee said:

> If it is successful it is the most completely satisfactory method of providing a substitute home.[26]

---

*Children Act 1975: the 'welfare principle' in Section 3 lays a duty upon courts and adoption agencies, in making any decision relating to the adoption of a child:
a) to have regard to all the circumstances, first consideration being given to the need to safeguard and promote the welfare of the child throughout his [or her] childhood; and
b) to ascertain as far as practicable the wishes and feelings of the child and give due consideration to them having regard to his [or her] age and under-standing.

The Act which followed the report, while not directly concerned with adoption, had profound implications for adoption practice because it established children's departments, with an expectation of developing professional expertise and the involvement of these local authority departments in adoption work. A further Adoption of Children Act was passed in 1949 which required a three-month probationary period before an adoption order was made, during which the placement would be supervised by the local authority, a provision which was already applicable to children placed by voluntary societies. The Act also enabled the adopted child to inherit as a member of the adoptive family rather than from the birth family, and also revised provisions relating to consents.

In the following year, 1950, a consolidating Act incorporated the four Acts dealing with adoption, and made amendments to the Adoption Act of 1926. These amendments allowed an adopted child to inherit property but not a title from adoptive parents. They also introduced the same consanguinity prohibitions as for biological children, thus ensuring that adopted children would not be allowed to marry close relatives within the adoptive family. Further, the ability to dispense with parental consent to adoption was introduced provided this could be shown to be unreasonably withheld. The latter suggested that the law was inclining to emphasise the rights of adopters rather than those of birth parents.

Thus from 1950 the British Isles had one Adoption Act, with certain modifications to conform to Scots law, the chief difference being that in Scotland (until 1964[27]) an adopted child continued to inherit from birth parents and they from him or her. The rights of adopted people over 17 in Scotland to have access to their birth records also remained.

The development of the organisation of the adoption service is itself an important study. Discussion and comment in the early reports seems to regard adoption as one of a range of options available to deprived children. Yet it developed as a separate activity, mainly the province of voluntary organisations or specialist sections in local authorities. It is tempting to speculate upon the reasons for that. Was it a hangover from the secrecy referred to in the Tomlin Report which conferred a mystique more imagined than real, or was it related to public attitudes to illegitimacy? Was it the desire of agencies to separate and protect the services to adopters and young single mothers from the pressures of other work so that they did not have to compete for scarce resources? Alternatively, did agencies feel that the legal and medical interface with social work adoption practice demanded specialist skills?

Whatever the reasons, adoption was substantially divorced from the mainstream of child care throughout the fifties and sixties. As subsequent sections will illustrate, a number of later developments influenced the direction of the organisation and place of adoption practice, culminating in the present position crystallised in the Children Act 1975 where adoption is clearly seen again as one of a range of services available for children deprived of the care of their own parents.

1950–1970: Consolidating and developing adoption in the welfare state

In January 1953, a further review of adoption was commissioned by the Home Office and the Scottish Department and a committee was appointed, under His Honour Sir Gerald Hurst 'to consider the present law relating to the adoption of children and to report whether any and, if so, what changes in policy or procedure are desirable in the interests of the welfare of children.'[28]

The principal recommendations included giving local authorities specific powers to arrange adoptions, and the inclusion of 'third parties' as respondents to the adoption. A further shift away from the rights of birth parents was illustrated by added powers to dispense with their consent. The role of the guardian *ad litem* was made more specific and judges were given added powers in situations where an application for an adoption order was refused.

The report further confirmed a belief in adoption, the 'general result' of which was said to have been 'to increase immeasurably the happiness and well-being of probably over a million members of the community'. It also expressed a firm conviction of the necessity for research into the outcome of adoption.

Telling the child

Of particular interest is the Hurst Committee decision to take evidence both on 'telling the child of his [or her] adoption' and on the 'origin of adopted persons'. The committee recorded a unanimous concern on the part of witnesses that adopted children *must* be told they are

17

adopted or 'chosen', and that this process should begin as early as possible. It seems clear that the committee felt that local authority and adoption society workers would explain the importance of these matters to would-be adopters. However, they seem equally convinced that in many adoptions, however well arranged and prepared, children are not told, and comment:

> At best there is a serious risk of totally destroying the child's trust and confidence in the adults who have been deceiving him [or her] about his [or her] parentage until then.

In an attempt to ensure that children were told of their adoption, the committee recommended that:

> a) an entry on the adoption application form should state that the child had been told of the application to adopt him [or her], or that the adopters undertake to bring him up in the knowledge that he is adopted;
> b) the Court is given a duty to ensure that the adopters have told or intend to tell the child of his [or her] adoption; and
> c) a memorandum on adoption should be given by the Court to the adopters, paying special attention to advice about the time and method of telling the child.

These concerns were dealt with in subsequent regulations[29] and circulars[30] as were the duties of the guardian *ad litem*.

The Home Office circular and explanatory memorandum for adopters was much more explicit on the point of adopters 'telling' the child of his or her adoption and origin. For example:

> When the Court considers your application for an adoption order, it will want to know whether the child is old enough to understand about adoption and, if so, whether you have told him [or her] about his application . . . It is best to decide to tell him as soon as he begins to ask questions, which is normally at the age of four or five. You can then gradually tell him more as he grows older. You may prefer not to tell him anything; but that would be unwise, because he would be likely to find out for himself sooner or later and if you had not told the discovery might be a great shock.[31]

While the intention of the committee was expressed, no machinery for enforcement was invoked and in the case of small children too young to understand at the time of the adoption order, the exercise of the right of the child to information on origins and adoption was left entirely to the adopters.

The adopted person's right to information

With regard to adopted people themselves obtaining information about their origins, the Hurst Committee paid particular attention to the discrepancy between English and Scottish Law. Scottish witnesses reported no problems arising from the provision allowing adopted persons over 17 to obtain information about themselves although some felt that the minimum age barrier should be raised to 21, a recommendation incorporated into the final report.[32]

Several English witnesses felt that the adopted person had a 'right' to the information and that it was 'not in the interest of adopted children to be permanently precluded from satisfying their natural curiosity', and that the same provision should be introduced in England and Wales.

Despite the general inclination of the committee to this view, it felt that there were practical difficulties and did not recommend accordingly. Instead the committee recommended that on reaching the age of 21 an adopted child should be able to obtain, from the court making the original adoption order, a full copy of that order. However, in the subsequent legislation[33] the age of enquiry in Scotland remained at 17 and a court order was still required in England and Wales to obtain such information.

In view of more recent experience it is interesting to consider in full some of the speculative comment of the Hurst Committee on the implication of a change in the law on this point:

> We have not overlooked that this recommendation might occasionally involve a risk of embarrassment for the natural mother of an illegitimate child, if the adopted person went so far as to seek her out. We believe, however, that most adopted persons would be content with the knowledge of their natural parentage, and would take no steps to make contact with their natural family – if, indeed, they could trace its present address – so that the risk would be slight and, in any event, it is one which we think that a mother who offers her child for adoption should be prepared to take.[34]

The Adoption Act 1958, which was based on the recommendations of the Hurst Committee, with its consequent rules and regulations[35] governed almost all aspects of adoption in this country for nearly 20 years.

In practice there also developed what McClean has called 'non law'.[36] Adoption agencies developed their own rules and selection criteria: even judges apparently succumbed to the temptation. It was reported to the Home Office in 1968 that since the Adoption Act 1958 received the Royal Assent some judges had been known to set their own age limits for adopters in addition to those laid down by the Act, and to demand a minimum period of marriage and evidence of infertility before considering an order. It was also recorded that a judge had refused to grant an application of a white couple to adopt a black child.[37]

In practice too it became clear that adoption arrangements were being made in a variety of ways – for example, by local authorities, by adoption agencies, by third parties (that is, intermediaries such as doctors, midwives, clergy and lawyers), and by mothers directly placing their children with someone wishing to adopt. Adoption also often developed from another set of circumstances such as long-term fostering, divorce and remarriage of parents, or a single parent with an illegitimate child adopting either singly or jointly with a spouse.

A survey of children placed for adoption in England and Wales in the years 1966/67/68/69[38] revealed that adoption placements by social work agencies averaged only approximately 50 per cent of the total, with local authorities making only approximately 15 per cent of those. Another survey conducted a little later showed that 58 per cent of placements were arranged by voluntary agencies and local authorities, four per cent were third party placements, nine per cent were direct placements and 30 per cent were applications made by a birth parent, usually jointly with a spouse.[39]

Given that such a large number of placements were privately arranged, it is not surprising that there was a long-standing controversy about whether the law should allow placements other than those made by bona fide agencies. In an overview of adoption literature, Jacka[40] comments on the sharp difference of opinion regarding the risks, or otherwise, involved in private adoption arrangements, and points out that the available research evidence is inconclusive. However, as we shall see later, third-party placement was eventually outlawed.

Organisational development and adoption practice

During this period, 1950–1970, there were other important developments in the field of professional social work and inevitably many of these were closely linked with the passing of legislation.

The recognition by the Curtis Committee of the need for trained and skilled workers in the field of child care was critical.[41] Such was their concern that they produced an interim report in 1946[42] which led to the establishment of the Central Training Council in Child Care in 1947 and special training courses. The Children Act 1948 created a specialist local authority department responsible for all children, which with trained workers would develop a professional understanding of the needs of deprived children. As mentioned earlier, the committee was favourably inclined towards adoption as a method of providing substitute care, but it also warned that closer supervision of adoption procedure was necessary. Adoption practice advanced on a somewhat erratic front and standards of work varied considerably, as recorded by Goodacre.[43]

Placements were made in a variety of ways and not all local authorities became involved in adoption work. Voluntary societies varied in standards of practice and many had organisational affiliations with implications for their adoption work. It was also suggested that local authorities did not satisfactorily exercise the function of registration and regulation of voluntary societies. Goodacre also reported a general reluctance on the part of children's officers to inspect, and particularly to penalise, colleagues in the voluntary sector.

In addition, it seems that adoption was not subject to Home Office inspection in the same way as other children's department functions.

Many voluntary societies, concerned about standards of work, formed the Standing Conference of Societies Registered for Adoption in 1950. This organisation became a forum for information and discussion and an important mouthpiece for adoption practitioners confirming, in its 1958 report, many of Goodacre's findings.[44] It is not surprising therefore that it also became a potent force in developing knowledge and skills in adoption practice. The organisation published a journal[45] and held regular national conferences. Importantly it also drew in medical practitioners (who formed their own group in 1963) and local authority representatives, not as members but as active participants.

Throughout the 1960s children's departments increasingly undertook adoption work.[46] It was therefore clearly a natural and necessary development that the local authorities should play a full part in any national organisation for those engaged in adoption work. To this end, in 1970, the Standing Conference of Societies Registered for Adoption became the Association of British Adoption Agencies, incorporating local authorities and voluntary agencies as full members, and affiliating the medical group.

Further progress in adoption practice was made by the publication of a report of a joint committee set up in 1967 by the advisory councils on child care in England, Wales and Scotland.[47] Practice standards were still variable and there was a generally accepted need to establish a base-line and framework for good adoption practice. The report attempted to do this drawing heavily from available research evidence. It also offered advice on the management and administration of an effective adoption service.

Before moving into the seventies the introduction of three further Adoption Acts should be noted. In 1960, making provision for the revocation of adoption orders in cases of legitimation; in 1964 recognising adoption orders made in the Channel Islands, Northern Ireland and the Isle of Man; and in 1968 dealing with international aspects of adoption and enabling courts to make orders under The Hague Convention on the adoption of children.[48]

The Seventies and Eighties
The decade from 1970 to 1980 could prove to be the most eventful in the history of adoption. In summary those ten years saw a major report on adoption;[49] major legislation affecting both adoption[50] and the organisation of social work services,[51] as well as a significant fluctuation in resources available to those services* and statistical changes in numbers and type of adoptions which in turn have been affected by changes in rates of illegitimacy, abortion, divorce and remarriage, and developments in birth control. There were also important developments in practice, with profound changes in

---

*The early years of the decade 1970–1980 saw rapid expansion in the personal social services, but in the latter part of the decade increasing financial restrictions were placed upon local authorities, first by the Labour government and from May 1979 by the Conservative government.

attitude to the questions of who may adopt and who may be adopted, stemming mainly from research findings and practice wisdom and experience here and overseas.

The departmental committee on the adoption of children chaired by Sir William Houghton, and later His Honour Judge Stockdale[52] was appointed in July 1969 to 'consider the law, policy and procedure on the adoption of children and what changes are desirable.' An unusual step for a committee of this kind was to produce an interim report or 'working paper',[53] the object of which was to 'enlist the help of all who have a personal or professional interest in adoption, and members of the public generally, in the Committee's work'.

The interim report provided a useful focus for the important issues in adoption law and practice which had developed in the 1960s[54] and which may be summarised thus:

1. Who should provide adoption services and what should be the extent and nature of those services? It was still felt that there was considerable variation in practice standards, and there was developing concern that the free giving of consent could only take place against a background of real choice, for example the availability of alternative methods of care and preventive strategies. Coupled with these concerns was the vexed question of direct and third party placements.

2. Who should be adopted, and for which children is adoption appropriate? There was concern that for some children adoption was not an appropriate mechanism, for example, illegitimate children adopted by birth parents; legitimate children adopted by birth parents; legitimate and illegitimate children adopted by one birth parent and one step-parent, and children adopted by their own relatives. On the other side of the coin was the strengthening conviction among practitioners that the approach to adoption should be more flexible. Consideration for adoption should be given to children who were older or of mixed race, who had physical and mental disabilities, or who languished in the care of local authorities with no real prospect of return to their parents and no experience of stable family life.*

3. How better to achieve the safeguarding of the child's interests?

---

*For example, the Adoption Resource Exchange, established in 1968, placed nine children in its first year and by 1971 was placing 74 children a year: all were older than the normal age for adoption, were of mixed parentage, or had physical or mental disabilities.

Social workers were concerned about the effectiveness of welfare supervision, and of the guardian *ad litem* role. Theoretically, three social workers could be, and often were, involved in an adoption: as the placement worker, as the supervising officer during the period that the child was protected, and as the guardian *ad litem*, the officer of the court. The second and third became involved at stages when it could be regarded as too late to achieve anything positive, unless the child was blatantly at risk. The functions of the guardian *ad litem* all involve processes and requirements which should be carried out by other workers at an earlier stage, and inevitably questions were raised about duplication, confusion to adopters, and fragmentation of responsibility. The problem was compounded by the view that the need for a guardian *ad litem* varied considerably according to how the placement was arranged. These very important issues were all raised in evidence by the Association of Child Care Officers.

4. To what extent should the welfare of the child be the major consideration? The Adoption Act of 1958 clearly states that 'the court before making an adoption order shall be satisfied that the order if made will be for the welfare of the child'.[55] The ACCO evidence wished to take this concept much further and make the child's welfare the 'first and paramount consideration' so that the child's right would be dominant in the proceedings and the rights of other parties would be subsidiary.[56] Questions of the child's rights also relate to issues discussed in paragraph 3 above and the inappropriate use of adoption merely to confer status or custody.

The themes highlighted in the Houghton inquiry were crystallised thus by Packman:

> Throughout all these changes and the varied responses of the statutory and voluntary administrators who influenced, or were influenced by them, three distinct but inter-related themes can be seen emerging. One concerns the balance between the rights of natural parents and the rights of adopters. A second relates to the quality of service to be offered to all parties to adoption which, in turn, affects some of the legal processes involved. The third concerns the appropriateness of adoption for children in a variety of circumstances . . . linking all three is the constant, but steadily more articulate concern to achieve what is in the best interests of the welfare of children.[57]

In its final form the Houghton Report ranged wider than the original terms of reference might seem to imply, and 92 recommendations went beyond specific comment upon adoption law and practice to consider guardianship and fostering. The overall effect was to put adoption firmly back in the mainstream of child care. The report also reaffirmed confidence in adoption as a concept and recommended that the law should continue to provide for the adoption of children.[58]

As might be expected of a radical document on an emotive subject, reactions to the Houghton interim report were strong and varied. The only point on which there appears to have been a consensus was that of the first consideration being given to the welfare of the child in the long term. This principle was embodied in the final report in relation to parental consent being unreasonably withheld, but it was stated much more forcefully in the Children Act 1975.

Most of the committee recommendations in fact passed into legislation.

The Children Act 1975
The Children Act 1975 received the Royal Assent on 12 November 1975, but implementation of much of it was very substantially delayed. Its most notable provisions were as follows: a duty on local authorities to provide a comprehensive adoption service as part of the general provision for children, and to include alternative resources and counselling for those with problems relating to adoption; 'third party' adoptions were placed outside the law; voluntary societies in future to be registered and inspected by central government; changes in criteria for those who may adopt, for example, the lower age limit was reduced to 21; a limited introduction of the concept of financial allowance to adopters; introduction of a new custodianship order; new arrangements for agreeing to adoption, changes in the criteria for dispensing with parental agreement, and new relinquishment and freeing procedures; changes in the arrangements for appointing a guardian *ad litem*; introduction of 'time limit' provisions in relation to the discharge of children from care; the extension of grounds for the assumption of parental rights; and arrangements for the retention of adoption records for 75 years.[59] Access to birth records for adopted people over the age of 18 years, which had also been a recommendation of the Houghton Committee, was included in the Act, and will be discussed in more detail in the next chapter.

Developments in professional practice

In professional practice the 1970s proved to be extremely active. The publication in 1973 of *Children who wait*, an important research study commissioned by the Association of British Adoption Agencies,[60] made a depressing impact upon many practitioners. It estimated that nationally there were approximately 7,000 children with 'special needs' waiting to be placed in a foster or adoptive home. It found that 40 per cent required 'permanent foster homes', five per cent needed direct adoption placement, 25 per cent needed a foster home with a view to adoption, and 28 per cent needed a foster home for an indeterminate period. Instead, the majority of these children would remain, in limbo, in local authority residential care. Major obstructions to placement were seen as: pressure of other work; poor recording and decision making; the behaviour and attitude of birth parents; a shortage of homes; and the abilities of foster parents. It also highlighted the blurring of boundaries between fostering and adoption, which found formal expression in early 1976 when the Association of British Adoption Agencies became the Association of British Adoption and Fostering Agencies, and the journal of the association became *Adoption & fostering* in issue number 2 of 1976. In an article published in that issue[61] the director of the association, Jane Rowe, wrote of the inter-relationship of fostering and adoption which had been 'emphasised' by the Children Act 1975, and of the final integration of adoption with other 'methods of serving children and their families' which should result.

Concern about fostering practice was acknowledged by central government in the setting up of a working party on fostering practice in 1974.[62] This had as its terms of reference: 'to compile a code of good fostering practice for the guidance of local authorities and voluntary organisations in boarding out children in their care, in the form of a guide which could be published for the use of social workers and others.' The code of practice produced by the working party was published in 1976.[63]

Many new initiatives developed in the 1970s were described by Cooper in a book published in 1978.[64] Predictably initiatives were generally directed towards the placement of children with special needs, but there were organisational developments too, and partici-pation was encouraged through the establishment of, for example, the National Foster Care Association in 1974, Parent-to-Parent Information on Adoption Services (a self-help group for adoptive parents) in 1971, and the National Association for the Childless in 1976. Various 'resource exchanges' also developed in different parts of the country* to facilitate the placing of children across greater distances than before, including the Adoption Resource Exchange. This subsequently negotiated a merger with the Association of British Adoption and Fostering Agencies, and the British Agencies for Adoption & Fostering (BAAF) was founded in 1981. In this context of change and development it seemed highly likely that the spirit of experiment and change which pervaded the 1970s would continue and even strengthen in the 1980s. This was despite the fact that the decade had a rather inauspicious start in this area with the publication of the Barclay Report on *Social workers, their role and tasks* in 1982.[65] Writing at the time, the editor of *Adoption & fostering*, the quarterly journal of BAAF, said those with an interest in work with children and family placement 'will gain as much guidance from Barclay as someone who asks a travel agent about holidays in Spain and is handed a train timetable'.[66] This important editorial went on to say that 'social work where children are concerned can no longer be a matter for vague generalisations or gentle dispute . . . It is now acknowledged that children are damaged if they grow up in care without a sense of the past or the future.'

At the time these reservations were being expressed, some major adoption issues of international concern were also developing. These divided delegates at the International Conference on Adoption at Eilat, Israel, in May 1982 and were rooted in the phenomenon of too few healthy babies for too many would-be adopters in the western world, and too many unwanted babies in the third world. The morality of inter-country adoption was, and continues to be, a major concern for many. The other main issue was described thus by Hedi Argent, who attended the conference: 'there was a distinct split between those who were entirely preoccupied with the supply and the demand for babies and those for whom adoption had moved from being a service for childless couples towards being a service for older and handicapped children. . . . At the same time there was a fairly fierce conflict between the gynaecologists and adoption workers about who is placing which

---

*For example, the Resource Exchange, South-East Scotland Resource Centre; the North Regional Children's Resource Exchange; the South-West Region Resource Exchange.

rare infant with which infertile couple.'[67] This debate highlighted the powerful motivation behind the formation of the National Association for the Childless and the impetus for perfecting medical techniques which would make the creation of families possible through human fertilisation and embryology. These will be discussed in more detail in chapter 5.

Transracial placements
Another major issue in the eighties has been that of transracial adoption. The British Adoption Project in the mid-sixties placed Afro-Caribbean, Asian and mixed-race children mainly with white families; follow-up studies were published in 1970 and 1976.[68] A BAAF research project on transracial adoption, which was funded by the DHSS and published in 1983,[69] produced further follow-up material and found that for a variety of reasons (and with some reservations) major difficulties did not occur in these adoptions. Many would disagree profoundly with these findings, as subsequent projects for the placement of black children* and many departmental placement policies would illustrate, and further research is urgently needed. The project, however, exposed a dilemma still facing some practitioners. The writers in an article summarising their project said: 'There is no doubt that for many black and mixed-race children placement with white parents is the only hope of achieving a permanent family of their own. The challenge for policy makers in the coming years is to combine the emphasis on black homes for black children with a recognition of the over-riding necessity of family placement for all those black, Asian and mixed-race children who require it.'[70] These views certainly do not find favour in all professional quarters and a thoughtful, concerned and sometimes emotional debate continues in which BAAF and NFCA are playing an important and constructive part.

Adoption allowances
The introduction of adoption allowances on an experimental basis in 1983 and of custodianship and freeing for adoption in 1984 made it possible for children for whom financial or complex legal situations had previously proved an insurmountable barrier to be adopted.

---

*For example, Soul kids, New black families. See also BAAF's Practice Note 13: The placement needs of black children, 1987.

Perhaps more controversially questions were asked about the need for adoption. For example, Sir Roger Ormrod, formerly judge in the Court of Appeal, asked in considering the permanent placement of older children: 'Is the change of status which adoption gives really worth all the trauma?'[71] Others argued that the absolute legal security of adoption was essential to the well-being of the child and the emotional security of the placement. The experience and opinions of the adopted people described in chapter 3 would not necessarily support that contention.

Open adoption

Related to the significant increase in the adoption of older children, and of children by their foster parents, was the issue of adoption with contact, or open adoption. This issue was explored by John Triseliotis in articles in 1983 and again in 1985.[72]

He put forward the notion that 'adoption with a condition of access should be an option to take account of a few children's meaningful attachments to members of their biological family'. He drew attention to the demographic and legal changes which challenge social workers to find adoptive families 'willing to tolerate contact between mainly older children and a member of their original family with whom they already have an attachment'. He also noted with concern the recent evidence that courts had been refusing adoption orders in cases where meaningful contacts existed but where in every other aspect adoption was deemed to be in the child's best interests.

Further exploration by the voluntary adoption agency Parents for Children was described by Hedi Argent in 1987.[73] In summarising the work with which she was associated, she pleaded for more openness within adoption to reflect the needs of the child. This openness may or may not include actual contact, but it recognises the need for information and knowledge about genetic inheritance in the process of growing up. For, as she says, 'some parents still find it hard to tell children that they are adopted or illegitimate'. She concluded with a comment from one family experiencing open adoption: 'We consider our son is a gift from his birth parents and not that we have rescued him from them.'

Counselling

In early 1988 the implementation of sections 1 and 2 of the Children

Act 1975 placed a duty on all local authorities to provide a comprehensive adoption service, to include 'counselling for persons with problems relating to adoption', thus recognising the complex interpersonal and emotional stresses associated with even successful adoptions.

Research findings
Development of the kind of service envisaged in the legislation demands proper consideration and informed pressure must be maintained to ensure that this happens. At the beginning of the previous decade Triseliotis voiced a fundamental concern about adoption practice which remains valid:

> Because adoption is an institution which does not exist in a void, it is essential for the practitioner to develop a frame of mind geared towards change. The survival of practice, and whether it continues to be in the hands of social workers, may be dependent upon how far the latter are prepared to look critically at their work, to view new concepts with an open mind and be ready to try innovations and use findings from research studies.[74]

Cooper's review[75] indicated that some social workers do appear to have an 'open mind' and are ready and able to explore new concepts. Whether they are ready to use research findings is perhaps less demonstrable, but as Cooper commented:

> It is the dearth of research, the lack of validation of findings, the small size of many samples and the nature of the sample chosen which taken together have failed to provide a reliable base for practice.

However, it would be inappropriate to ignore the substantial and helpful research which has been produced since 1970, notably by Kadushin[76] and Jaffee *et al*[77] in 1970; Crellin *et al*[78] and Raynor[79] in 1971; Seglow *et al*[80] in 1972; Triseliotis[81] in 1973 and with Russell[82] in 1984; Tizard[83] in 1979; Raynor[84] in 1980; Rowe *et al*[85] in 1984; Millham *et al*[86] in 1985; Packman *et al*[87] in 1986; Maluccio *et al*[88] in 1986; and Wilson[89] in 1987. Some of the findings in these collected works indicate the following: that agencies may take risks in placing older children with a high probability of success; that adopted children perform developmentally rather better than illegitimate children who remain with their own families; that adopted children tend to fare better than children in long-term care who have been restored to their families; that adopters and adopted children need considerably more help regarding the method and timing of the revelation of adoptive status; and that adopted people's need to know about their genealogical background and the circumstances of their adoption is an extremely potent force.

Perhaps this research has raised more issues than it has resolved. Towards the end of the seventies Cooper summarised what she called the four key questions which continued to exercise policy makers and practitioners, and which required searching and substantial investigation.[90] These were, and are:

1. In what kind of circumstances and for what category of children is either long-term fostering or adoption the treatment of choice?

2. If it is established that family placement is appropriate as the preferred form of treatment, then is adoption so much more emotionally secure than fostering that a move towards adoption is justified?

3. Is a shift of resources required in order to ensure that there is a heavy investment in restoration, immediately after parental separation and during the first year, so that early restoration in reality becomes a basic goal for the majority of children, however and wherever placed?

4. If restoration is found to be impracticable or even damaging, is it then important to make a decision and plan for permanence in placement?

These four questions will, one suspects, long continue to underpin thought and development in both adoption and fostering. It is perhaps a pious hope that, at times of financial stringency in the public sector, either research or implementation of the existing legislation will receive sympathetic treatment in the allocation of resources; perhaps much will depend upon the ability of practitioners to draw public attention to the dangers of carrying out practices which profoundly affect the lives of children without proper evaluation taking place at the same time.

Against this background it seems particularly relevant to record the actual experiences and views of adopted people: chapter 3 seeks to do this.

The Children Act 1989 received royal assent on 16 November 1989 and will be implemented in late 1991. It is undoubtedly, as described by the relevant government departments in the introduction to the Act published by HMSO, 'the most comprehensive piece of legislation which Parliament has ever enacted about children'. It strikes a new balance between family autonomy and the protection of children and will make even greater demands upon the time and skills of those working in the field of child care.

References

1 Cooper J D *Patterns of family placement – current issues in adoption and fostering* National Children's Bureau, 1978.

2 McWhinnie A *Adopted children, how they grow up* Routledge & Kegan Paul, 1966.

3 Triseliotis J *Evaluation of adoption policy and practice* University of Edinburgh, 1970.

4 Heywood J S *Children in care* Routledge & Kegan Paul, 1987.

5 Ellison M *The adopted child* Gollancz, 1958.

6 Report of the committee on child adoption (Cmnd 1254) HMSO, 1921.

7 Child adoption committee: first report (Cmnd 2401) HMSO, 1925;
Second report (Cmnd 2469) HMSO, 1926;
Third report (Cmnd 2711) HMSO, 1926.

8 Heywood J S *Services for children and their families* Pergamon, 1973.

9 Hansard, 6 March 1872, col 1486.

10 Infant Life Protection Acts 1872 and 1897.

11 Registration of Births and Deaths Act 1874;
Notification of Births Acts 1907 and 1913.

12 Prevention of Cruelty to and Protection of Children Act 1889;
Prevention of Cruelty to Children (Amendment) Act 1894.

13 Packman J *The child's generation* Basil Blackwell & Martin Robertson, 1975.

14 Eventually formalised in the Boarding out of Children Regulations 1955 and the Boarding out of Children (Foster Placement) Regulations 1988.

15 See 4 above.

16 Education and maintenance of pauper children in the metropolis (C 8027), 1896. Reported in Heywood (4 above).

17 Rowe J and Lambert L *Children who wait* ABAA, 1973.

18 See 8 above.

19 See 6 above.

20 One bill in 1922; two bills in 1923; three bills in 1924; two bills in 1925.

21 See 7 above.

22 Adoption of Children Act 1926.

23 Adoption of Children (Scotland) Act 1930.

24 Report of the departmental committee on adoption societies and agencies (Cmnd 5499) HMSO, 1937.

25 Adoption Society Regulations 1943.

26 Report on the care of children committee (Cmnd 6922) HMSO, 1946.

27 The Succession (Scotland) Act 1964.

28 Report of the departmental committee on the adoption of children (Cmnd 9248) HMSO, 1954.

29 Adoption (County Court) Rules, second schedule, 1959.

30 Home Office letter HO 53/59, 1959.

31 Explanatory memorandum to be given to applicants for adoption orders, sent to local authorities with 30 above.

32 See 28 above.

33 Adoption Act 1958.

34 See 28 above.

35 Adoption Agencies Regulations 1959; Adoption (County Court) Rules 1959; Adoption (Juvenile Court) Rules 1959; Adoption (High Court) Rules 1971.

36 McClean J D *The legal context of social work* Butterworth, 1975.

37 See 36 above.

38 Lambert L 'Adoption, the statistical picture' *Child adoption* 63, 1969.

39 Gray E and Blunden R *A survey of adoption in Great Britain* HMSO, 1971.

40 Jacka A A *Adoption in brief: research and other literature in the United States, Canada and Great Britain 1966–72* NFER, 1973.

41 See 26 above.

42 Training in child care: interim report of the care of children committee (Cmnd 6760) HMSO, 1946.

43 Goodacre I *Adoption policy and practice* Allen and Unwin, 1966.

44 Report of the standing conference of societies registered for adoption, 1958.

45 *Child adoption,* later *Adoption & fostering.*

46 *Report of the departmental committee on the adoption of children* (Cmnd 5107) HMSO, 1972.

47 *A guide to adoption practice* HMSO, 1970.

48 Convention on jurisdiction, applicable law and recognition of decrees relating to adoption: final act of tenth session of the Hague Conference on Private International Law (Cmnd 2613) HMSO, 1964.

49 See 46 above.

50 Children Act 1975.

51 Local Authority Social Services Act 1970.

52 See 46 above. Chaired by Sir William Houghton until his death on 16 November 1971. His Honour Judge Stockdale was appointed chair on 1 December 1971.

53 'Adoption of children: working paper containing provisional proposals by the departmental committee on the adoption of children' HMSO, 1970.

54 'Adoption – the way ahead' ACCO Monographs, 1969.

55 Adoption Act 1958, section 7(b).

56 See 54 above.

57 See 13 above.

58 See 46 above.

59 Adoption Agencies Regulations, 1976.

60 See 17 above.

61 Rowe J 'Adoption and fostering – a combined service' *Adoption & fostering* 84 2, 1976.

62 Set up by the DHSS, the Scottish Education Department (Social Work Services Group) and the Welsh Office.

63 *Foster care – a guide to practice* HMSO, 1976.

64 See 1 above.

65 *Social workers, their roles and tasks* (Report of a working party set up in October 1980 at the request of the Secretary of State for Social Services by the National Institute for Social Work, Chair: Peter Barclay) Bedford Square Press, 1982.

66 Editorial (Sarah Curtis) *Adoption & fostering* 6 3, 1982.

67 Argent H 'International conference on adoption' (Newspoint) *Adoption & fostering* 6 3, 1982.

68 Raynor *Adoption of non-white children in Britain* Allen and Unwin, 1970; Jackson B *Family experiences of inter-racial adoption* ABAFA, 1976.

69 Gill O and Jackson B *Adoption and race: black, Asian and mixed race children in white families* BAAF/Batsford, 1983.

70 Gill O and Jackson B 'Transracial adoption in Britain' *Adoption & fostering* 6 3, 1982.

71 Ormrod Sir R 'Child care law: a personal perspective' *Adoption & fostering* 94, 1985.

72 Triseliotis J 'Identity and security in adoption and long-term fostering' *Adoption & fostering* 7 1, 1983; 'Adoption with contact' *Adoption & fostering* 9 4, 1985.

73 Argent H 'Progress in open adoption' *Adoption & fostering* 11 2, 1987.

74 Triseliotis J *Evaluation of adoption policy and practice* University of Edinburgh, 1970.

75 See 1 above.

76 Kadushin A *Adopting older children* New York: Columbia University Press, 1970.

77 Jaffee B and Fanshel D *How they fared in adoption: a follow up study* New York: Columbia University Press, 1970.

78 Crellin E, Pringle MLK and West P *Born illegitimate: social and educational implications* NFER, 1971.

79 Raynor L *The adoption of non-white children* Allen and Unwin, 1971.

80 Seglow J, Pringle MLK and Wedge P *Growing up adopted: a long-term national study of adopted children and their families* NFER, 1972.

81 Triseliotis J *In search of origins* Routledge & Kegan Paul, 1973.

82 Triseliotis J and Russell J *Hard to place: the outcome of adoption and residential care* Heinemann Educational, 1984.

83 Tizard B *Adoption: a second chance* Open Books, 1977.

84 Raynor L *The adopted child comes of age* Allen and Unwin, 1980.

85 Rowe J, Cain H, Hundleby M and Kean A *Long-term foster care* BAAF/ Batford, 1984.

86 Millham S, Bullock R, Hosie K and Haak M *Lost in care: the problems of maintaining links between children in care and their families* Gower, 1986.

87 Packman J, Randall J and Jacques N *Who needs care? Social work decisions about children* Basil Blackwell, 1986.

88 Maluccio A, Fein E and Olmstead A *Permanency planning for children: concepts and methods* Tavistock, 1986.

89 Wilson A *Mixed race children: a study of identity* Unwin Hyman, 1987.

90 See 1 above.

2 Access to birth records: development in England & Wales

Section 26 [of the Children Act 1975] gives effect to the recommendation of the Houghton Committee that adopted people who have reached the age of 18 should be entitled to a copy of their original birth certificate. It reflects the view which is now widely accepted and taken account of in adoption practice that an adopted child, if he [or she] is to develop a proper sense of identity, need to know that he was adopted and should be given information to satisfy his natural curiosity about his origin.[1]

This chapter will outline the development of 'access to birth records' in England and Wales and explore some of the professional, philosophical and parliamentary thinking which underpinned the eventual change in the law.

The central government statement quoted above encompasses, yet disguises, many profound issues which have been debated at length over the years but which are still largely unresolved. Arising as they do from fundamental questions surrounding identity, infertility, illegitimacy, biological and social parenting, and human rights, it is not surprising, as Jane Rowe wrote in 1970, that 'no really adequate philosophic base has been developed for the adoptive family'.[2]

In the same article Rowe draws attention to the lack of discussion about what adoption really is, to the conflict between the legal and administrative certainties about adoption, and to the cultural doubts exemplified by distinctions drawn between 'own' and 'adopted' children, and 'real' – meaning biological – parents as opposed to adoptive parents.

Developing the theme Rowe discusses at some length the significant limitations in our language, reflecting and perpetuating the general lack of understanding and acceptance of the complex family relationships implicit in the state of adoption. She finds social workers too guilty of a lack of clarity and sensitivity:

Available adjectives, such as 'biological' and 'natural', are clumsy and unsatisfactory or they have implicit value judgments, such as 'own' or 'real'. But the distinction between 'own' and 'adopted' is in such general use even by social workers that its denigrating, almost insulting, connotation passes unnoticed except by those who are wounded by it. Subtly but surely it perpetuates the notion that the adopted child is not quite so much a part of the family as if he [or she] were born into it. He has to earn his place.

Telling children about their origins

There would appear to be little evidence that the problems outlined by Rowe have decreased. They are further compounded by the difficulties of giving adopted children information about their origins – difficulties which Rowe claimed were 'seriously underestimated' by social workers, and 'rightly' perceived by adopters as acts which set in motion 'complex and emotion-laden wheels'. She also suggested that while many would agree that adoptive parents need education for their special tasks, few actually received such help. Neither practitioners nor the many then available booklets[3] for substitute parents really engaged with what Rowe called 'the double bind of "make this child your own but tell him that he isn't"'.

This important article by the then director of the Association of British Adoption Agencies, written at a time when the Houghton Committee was in session, would seem to suggest significant unresolved and unsatisfactory areas of adoption practice. The theoretical framework of adoption has certainly developed and become more enlightened;[4,5] areas of practice have also improved, such as the selection of applicants and the placement of children hitherto considered unsuitable.[6,7,8,9] However, whilst most practitioners would endorse the view that adopted people should be given relevant information about their origins, and despite the pioneering work of the Post-Adoption Centre and BAAF, the practice skills directed towards helping adopters to handle the question of 'telling' would appear to have advanced little. It is of course significant that practitioners are afforded very few relevant opportunities to work helpfully with adopters on this issue because of the nature and timing of their involvement, a factor which may change now that Section 1 of the Children Act 1975 has been implemented.*

The need to know

A major task faced by adopted people is the development of a sense of separate identity out of what Sants in 1967 called 'genealogical bewilderment'.[10] Triseliotis in 1974 posed the question of 'how far adopted people face similar or different developmental tasks from those who have not been adopted'.[11] These 'growing-up' tasks may be seen as achieving a mature independence and a clear sense of identity, and being able to give and receive love. They are inextricably linked with knowledge and feelings about heritage and about how other people see us and behave towards us.

Thus while the growing-up tasks may be common to all, the adopted person's development may be hampered by lack of knowledge. Margaret Kornitzer described the situation graphically in 1971 when writing of the effect upon the adopted person's natural development of a sense of identity when there has been a failure to provide information about 'blood and bones':

> Background knowledge of one's family is like baby food – it is literally fed to a person as part of the normal nourishment that builds up his [or her] mental and emotional structure and helps the person to become acquainted with what he [or she] is so that he can seize his inheritance of himself.[12]

She goes on to discuss the importance of knowing what our (biological) parents were like in understanding much about ourselves, and of the reality being 'healthier' than the fantasy. The point is made that simply being honest with adopted children is not enough: 'Even those adopted children whose adopters have been quite honest with them do feel left out on a limb at a certain point in their development, because they can have no visual or mental picture of the couple who gave them their physical continuity in the chain of life'; a fact denied by many practitioners and adopters.

At a more mundane level, as McWhinnie reports,[13] the simplest tasks of adult life, such as completing medical data on forms, can become an ordeal because of the adopted person's lack of very basic

---

*This states that 'it will be the duty of local authorities to establish a comprehensive adoption service for all parties associated with adoption, including a counselling service for persons with problems relating to adoption'.

information about biological background which others possess as a matter of course.

An adopted person has, in Triseliotis' view, to base his or her identity on 'the concept of two sets of parents'.[14] Rowe,[15] Kirk,[16] Triseliotis[17] and Rosner[18] agree that adopters need to feel and experience the child as their own, and have confidence in the validity of their family. Jan de Hartog, a novelist and adopter, goes as far as to say that the adoptive mother should totally exclude the birth mother for a time in order to make the child her own.[19]

The crucial issue, says Rowe, is that adopters should not pretend that being an adoptive parent is the same as being a biological parent, but should have a 'sturdy belief that their form of parenthood really is parenthood'. They also need to be able to feel 'some sense of kinship with the people who gave their child birth', and truly absorb the child's background into their family traditions.

In the Triseliotis study of 1973,[20] adopted people identified many important elements of the growing-up task, the first being acceptance of the loss of birth parents and the rejection that this suggests.

For children from different racial or cultural backgrounds from their adopters there is also the task of incorporating aspects of the two cultures and of knowing where they stand in the world.

Adolescence is generally a period of confusion and search for identity which is heightened for adopted persons. It is a commonly-held view (see Erikson[21]) that all adolescents need to know about and understand the past before being able to manage the future.

Triseliotis[22] also underlined the fact that inherent in the adoptive state is a risk to the development of security and belonging because, as Kornitzer has stated: 'with adopted people a mystery actually exists'.[23] However, the more important issue is surely how the child is made to feel within the family, the security of roles and relationships, and the openness and trust which exists. Indeed, Kadushin's work has clearly demonstrated the ability of a secure, loving setting to reverse the effects of trauma in children.[24]

Attitudes in the outside world

Unfortunately, as Triseliotis illustrated, the problems encountered by adopted persons in the maturation process are not limited to the resolution of attitudes, roles and relationships within the family. The community too has a subtle but profound effect: 'However successful adoptive parents are in their parental task, they cannot protect the child from the nuances of the outside world'.[25] He also refers to 'covert negative messages', which are best illustrated by some of his examples from discussion with adopted people:

> When I told my fiancé I was adopted his reply was 'I do not know what my father and mother will feel . . .'

> When my boy was born and my mother-in-law visited me in hospital she exclaimed: 'Thank God that he has taken from our side of the family.' I know what she was getting at and it hurt.

> Somehow I felt that my parents were ashamed to talk about it and they gave me the feeling that adoption was unnatural . . .

This rather horrifying commentary on the attitudes of outsiders towards adoption is not something we may conveniently dismiss as a thing of the past. There can be little doubt that adopted people today face similar attitudes and experiences. Indeed, as the numbers of adoptions have reduced significantly over the years (from a total of 22,373 in England and Wales in 1970, to a total of 12,121 in 1978 and 7,892 in 1986), the corresponding reduction of personal experience of adoption may have led to even greater ignorance and insensitivity than hitherto.

Thus the concept of access to birth records must be considered against a shifting foundation of confusion about the real nature of adoption. On the one hand we have absolute legal precision about the status of adoption and on the other, highly complex cultural and emotional uncertainty. It is in this context, and that of the complicated development of maturity and independence, that adopted people seek information on, and sometimes direct contact with, their origins.

Obviously the attitudes, real or perceived, of adoptive parents and the wider community will have a profound influence on adopted people, who will be torn between feelings of guilt and disloyalty and the genealogical bewilderment which Sants has said may stimulate a 'relentless pursuit of the facts of their origin'.[26]

Developments leading to access to birth records: 1926–1975
At this point it is worth tracing the development from the Adoption Act 1926 to the Children Act 1975, which resulted in the right of adopted people aged 18 and over in England and Wales to have copies of their original birth certificate.[27]

41

A useful starting point is the first committee of inquiry into adoption in 1921[28] which at least recognised the importance of the original parent/child relationship by encouraging preventive effort. However, it is not surprising that little consideration was given to links with the original family at a time when attention was focused on the complicated question of establishing legal adoption for the first time in this country.

More significantly, the Tomlin Committee[29] which sat between 1925 and 1926, commented adversely upon the then common placement practice of agencies to 'seek to fix a gulf between the child's past and future'. Reference has already been made to the relevant sections of the Adoption Act 1926 and the Adoption of Children (Scotland) Act 1930.

As outlined earlier, the Hurst Committee[30] which reported in 1954 did take evidence on the child's need to know about his or her origins, and considered these issues in considerable detail. Its report also made recommendations to ensure that the child was told of his or her adoption. However, no legal enforcement of the recommendation was made and the right of the adopted child to be given information on his or her origins was left substantially in the hands of the adopters who, in turn, were dependent upon the information others were prepared to give them. The committee's report alluded to 'practical difficulties' which could arise if the same provision were to be extended to England and Wales but did not specify these. Indeed, the relevant paragraphs all seem to indicate that the committee and its witnesses were quite strongly of the view that measures *should* be introduced to enable adopted persons to satisfy their natural curiosity about their origins. In practice, however, nothing changed, although doubtless the process of taking and considering evidence has some influence over future thinking.

With the considerable developments in child care organisation and practice since 1948 it is hardly surprising that theoreticians and practitioners became more aware of the significance of the biological parent to the separated child. Whether the ultimate plan was rehabilitation with parents, or whether the placement was permanent and the parents hidden or even anonymous, they were increasingly seen as a potent force in the child's healthy development, as the writings of Bowlby,[31] Pringle,[32] Rowe[33] and McWhinnie[34] testify.

The Houghton Report

This developing climate of opinion was the background to what has become popularly known as the Houghton Report,[35] published in 1972. The committee which was set up in July 1969 took the somewhat unusual step of publishing a working paper as a basis for discussion in October 1970.[36] This was intended to elicit focused comment from all interested parties. In addition to the working paper, the committee commissioned research on various topics, including a study of 'the use made in Scotland of the provision in Scottish adoption law for an adopted person to have access to his original birth record'. This important piece of research was carried out by John Triseliotis[37] and was clearly a significant influence upon the recommendations made in the final report. At the time of the publication of the working paper the committee was of the view that the law affecting access to birth records should remain unchanged in England and Wales, and should be reviewed in Scotland in the light of the research. By the final report this view had altered significantly.

The aims of the study as set out by Triseliotis were 'to identify the general circumstances of adopted adults who seek information about their origins; to establish their reasons for the search, their motivation, their needs and objectives and also to what use they put the information gained'.

The 70 people interviewed fell into two distinct groups: those who wanted to find either or both of their birth parents, and those who simply wanted to obtain background information. The former group was the more strongly motivated. It comprised 42 people, or 60 per cent of the sample, and four had actually traced their birth parents, while a further seven had been able to contact blood relations. Sixty-five per cent of the sample were aged 11 or over when they discovered they were adopted, and 30 per cent had been told by their adopters, the others having discovered by chance. Significantly, 65 per cent of the sample felt immediately that their search for information had been helpful, and four months later 90 per cent had no regrets about their actions.

Other evidence presented to the committee was conflicting: for example, members of the Association of British Adoption Agencies[38] reported 'a considerable division of opinion' which seemed to reflect quite strongly the existing laws and practice in Scotland and in England and Wales. The medical group of the association strongly endorsed the view that adopted children should be given as much background information as possible, but also stated:

> We do not find any evidence that the well-being of the child required him [or her] to know the names of his natural parents or to make contact with them and in view of the undesirable possibilities such a facility would raise agree that it should only be granted by the courts in very exceptional circumstances and after an adoption agency has adequately counselled the applicant and provided a report to the court.

However, the records of the Registrar General for Scotland did not apparently yield any record of complaints from birth relatives and the committee concluded that the 'fear of being traced may therefore have been unduly magnified', and that as the social climate was changing, 'mothers are becoming less concerned to conceal the fact that they have had an illegitimate child.'[39]

As a further argument the report also quoted a National Children's Bureau study[40] in which 53 per cent of adoptive parents felt that adoptive children should be allowed free access to their original records.

The conclusion of the committee was that 'the weight of the evidence as a whole was in favour of freer access to background information, and this accords with our wish to encourage greater openness about adoption.' They therefore recommended that:

> arrangements should be made for the preservation of adoption records for 75 years;

and

> an adopted person aged 18 years or over should be entitled to a copy of his [or her] original birth certificate.

The committee naturally felt that the Scottish arrangements should continue, but that the age for access to birth records should be brought into line with what was recommended for England and Wales, ie raised to 18.

Comments were made in discussion on some of the details of practical arrangements. Whilst generally approving the arrangements made by the Registrar General in Scotland, the committee clearly felt that adopted people seeking information would require more than mere facts. They concluded that many would need help and information in dealing with problems of identity and that this should be offered by the relevant adoption agency or local authority social services department. The committee also considered the question of access to court records and concluded that this should be at the discretion of the court and not an automatic right, as was then the case in Scotland.

The fact that the committee was explicit about the control of disclosure of court records but not of agency records is of interest, but as no explanation is given the significance is unclear. It was not within the scope of the present study to examine court attitudes although this would appear to warrant further investigation. The impression gained from respondents is that court personnel were often unclear about their role and responsibilities, and the variety of responses did not appear to be based upon any established policy or criteria for the exercise of discretion.

Recommendation 77 of the Houghton Committee prompted a great deal of public debate, controversy, and at times near-hysteria. There were television programmes and newspaper articles expressing every possible point of view with varying degrees of accuracy. However, the most comprehensive and balanced summary of the arguments is probably the record of parliamentary consideration of the government-sponsored Children Bill which received its first reading on 12 December 1974. This discussion inevitably represented not only the personal views of members influenced by individual lobbying, but also the official submissions of professional groups such as the Association of Directors of Social Services and the British Association of Social Workers.

The Children Bill debate

Dr David Owen, who introduced the second reading of the bill, referred to Clause 25 (access to birth records), and commented that adopted people had a right to know their true identity, that there was no evidence of real problems from the Scottish experience and that it was already possible, though difficult, to obtain information in England and Wales. He also warned that there could be 'one or two cases which will cause distress'. Of the 15 other speakers in the debate, five made explicit reference to Clause 25:

Mr Leo Abse, Chairman from 1964 to 1969 of the inter-party committee on adoption law review and member of the Houghton

Committee, supported the clause. He spoke of the 'syndrome of genealogical bewilderment' which simply expressed the need to answer the question 'who am I?'. He also argued for the need to try and mitigate unfortunate consequences by the involvement of some kind of social agency.

Mr Emlyn Hooson, himself an adopter as he announced in the chamber, also strongly supported clause 25, stating that it embodied an 'absolute right' of adopted people.

Mrs Jill Knight, who referred to information received from a friend in the National Adoption Society, spoke of grave reservations, disastrous consequences and the possibilities of blackmail. She said that there could be no statistical proof of worry and commented that no person should be given the right to 'wreck another person's life'. She gave notice of her intention to move amendments. Mrs Lynda Chalker was supportive of clause 25 and made the point that those determined to find out about their origins will probably do so anyway. She felt strongly, however, that an adoption agency should be involved, and was firmly of the view that the legislation should not be made retrospective, a point strongly supported by the Association of Directors of Social Services and one which was to be the focus of much disagreement.

Mr Philip Whitehead, himself adopted by a private arrangement and who had met his birth mother when he was 30, spoke of the adopted person wishing to become psychologically whole, and wanting to know who and what he or she is. He stressed however that this did not embrace the desire to create another 'substantial familial relationship'. In accepting that problems and trauma may be inherent in the situation he felt that counselling should be available to the adopted person. He also made the point that approaching marriage could often trigger off the desire for genealogical information. He made the only comment suggesting that access to birth records could have positive connotations for birth families, stating that birth parents too could often feel deprived and yet were unable to obtain information which might help them.

The bill was then committed to a standing committee[41] chaired by Richard Crawshaw, which had 27 members and sat on 14 occasions between 1 July 1975 and 5 August 1975.

Clause 25 was considered during the seventh and eighth sittings which were held on 17 July and 22 July. Mrs Jill Knight introduced an amendment at an early stage in the standing committee discussion, the effect of which would be to make the provisions of clause 25 available only to those adopted on or after 1 August 1975. This prompted a long debate about retrospective legislation before the amendment was finally withdrawn with notice that it might be raised again at the report stage. The discussion revolved around: the balance between rights of the adopted person and the birth parents; civil rights in relation to retrospective legislation, especially as birth parents would have been assured that they could not be identified in future except in rare circumstances; the potentially disastrous effects upon a marriage where one partner had not divulged the fact that he/she had, in the past, placed a child for adoption; responsibilities of legislators to those with problems of identity; the problem of the 'psychopathic' adopted person and the effect of his or her pursuit of birth parents; and the serious concerns of adopters about the effects of their adopted children actively seeking information about their origins. Several references were made to the relatively trouble-free Scottish experience and the fact that no complaints had been received by the Registrar General in Scotland.

Finally Dr Owen encapsulated the spirit of the intention of the members in his summary of this part of the discussion. He felt that Parliament must legislate for a balance of rights, and a balance of 'unknown' distress and anxiety with 'known' distress to a large number of people currently excluded from the right to basic information about themselves. In order to satisfy the wish of the majority he suggested that the right to have access to birth records should be established, but that reasonable precautions should also be taken – ie access to counselling.

In subsequent consultation on this topic, it was clear that many agencies supported the idea of a combination of available counselling agencies, and that directors of social services were unhappy about the notion of one centralised unit. It was also noted that a body of social work opinion was uneasy about the concept of obligatory counselling.

The Houghton Report was not particularly enlightening upon the extent and nature of the proposed counselling, and not surprisingly the parliamentary discussion also reflected some concern and confusion about the form this would take. At the same time however, members repeatedly stressed the need for counselling.

On 28 October 1975 the bill received its third reading and was passed by royal assent on 12 November 1975. The final wording gives

47

adopted people over 18 the right to information about their birth records and lays a duty on local authorities and adoption societies to provide counselling. Those adopted before 12 November 1975 were required to see a counsellor before being given the information they sought. Those adopted on or after 12 November 1975 should be offered the opportunity to see a counsellor if they wished, but need not do so. Applicants may select one of the following to provide a counsellor:

i) the Registrar General's office;
ii) the applicant's local authority;
iii) the local authority in whose area the adoption order was made; or
iv) the adoption society which arranged the adoption, provided it is approved.

Section 26 (as it was enacted) also enables adopted people under 18 who are intending to marry to apply to the Registrar General for any information in their records about whether they and the person they intend to marry come within the prohibited degree of relationship for marriage.

As stated previously, implementation of this section took place on 26 November 1976 and the central government circular, giving detailed guidance on implementation, was issued during the same month.[42] It outlines the procedures to be followed and explains the counselling arrangements made by the Registrar General. Perhaps the most interesting aspect of the circular is that for the first time an attempt is made to consider some of the detailed implications of counselling. The circular states that counselling will require 'skill and maturity' and 'experience of work with families', as well as 'familiarity with adoption practice and procedures'. It suggests also that local authorities may wish to arrange for the work to be done on a sessional basis by voluntary agencies or retired social workers.

It was anticipated that applicants would fall into three main categories: those requiring very specific and limited information; those wanting full information but no contact with birth parents; and those hoping to trace and meet one or both of their parents.

The purpose of counselling is seen as ensuring that the applicant has fully considered the effects of his or her enquiries and that they are provided with information. The role of counselling is seen as clarifying objectives, helping to find and understand information, and minimising problems both by the application of social work skills and by acting as an intermediary when appropriate. It is therefore obvious that those social workers allocated to counselling work should possess social work skills and knowledge of a high order, as well as a detailed knowledge of adoption legislation and practice. A working knowledge of record-keeping procedures in a variety of settings including the General Register Office also seems important. This counselling service needs to be accessible and available, implying for its workers the absence of a high level of crisis work or an excessive case-load. While these conditions are desirable for all those seeking a social work service, they would seem crucial for those who may be ambivalent about what has brought them to a social work agency and confused about their own image and identity.

Findings following implementation

Since 26 November 1976, when Section 26 of the Children Act 1975 inserted a new Section 20A in the Adoption Act 1958 and legislated for access to birth records for adopted persons, there have been three published surveys of the operation of the new provision.

The first was carried out by Alfred Leeding[43] in 13 local authorities, mainly in the West Midlands. The survey was commissioned by the Association of British Adoption and Fostering Agencies, and the director of the association pointed out in the foreword that it had been felt appropriate to undertake some immediate evaluation of the effects of the legislation. The association had been highly involved in earlier discussion and presentation of evidence, and wished now to provide information to members, the government and the many questioners from overseas interested in the British experience. The survey was carried out in the first four months following implementation and Leeding writes of the 'consternation all around' about this controversial procedure. Even the normally sober *Daily Telegraph* printed headlines such as 'Fear of emotional upsets over "reveal-all" adoption law' (11 October 1976). Maximum publicity accompanied the survey.

A total of 279 people were included in the survey and the major findings were as follows:

seven out of ten applicants were women;

46 per cent of applicants were in the 30–39 age group;

39 per cent were adopted between the ages of six and 11 months;

34 per cent were adopted during the war years.

Much of the other information is inevitably impressionistic or based on what applicants volunteered. It must therefore be treated with a little caution, but is nonetheless informative. For example, approximately 20 per cent wished to seek out a parent, and 11 of these are known to have succeeded. More than 50 per cent simply wanted information about their early history but did not want to make contact.

The adoptive parents of approximately 20 per cent of the applicants had died and, of those living, approximately one couple in seven were said to be supporting, or at least not opposing, the application.

Other findings were:

seven per cent of applicants wanted to find out about a medical condition thought to have been inherited;

two per cent wanted to clarify their racial origin: one of these wished to marry and the acceptable ethnic origin was crucial to the marriage taking place;

14 per cent recalled unkind or unfavourable experiences relating to their adoptive state;

15 per cent spoke of their adoption as a happy experience;

both groups, however, wanted information on their origins;

seven people gave counsellors cause for concern.

In general, Leeding felt that his survey showed that the majority of those wishing to meet their parents are responsible and sensitive.

The second survey[44] was based upon the first 500 interviews carried out at the General Register Office in London and was carried out on behalf of the Secretaries of State for Social Services and for Wales. It was based upon information gathered and recorded by counsellors and differed from Leeding's survey in that some specific questions were put for purposes of the research.

Of the 500 people interviewed, 58 per cent were women and nearly 50 per cent were in the 25–34 age group. The other main findings were as follows:

access to birth records was of positive personal significance for a large number;

fewer than 30 per cent had been well and helpfully told of their adoption status;

those interviewed felt strongly that they had 'the right to know' and generally approved of the arrangements including counselling; there was compassionate and sensitive understanding of the birth mother's position;

for 53 per cent of applicants (130 men and 187 women) the prime motivation was the need to establish or complete a sense of 'true self-identity';

16 per cent appear to have been motivated by curiosity;

at the time of interview 28 per cent intended to trace a birth parent, 39 per cent said they did not intend to trace and 33 per cent were unsure;

22 per cent of applicants were felt to have damaging adverse factors in their adoptive experience, the most damaging a breakdown in normal communications within the family;

applicants with unhappy adoption experiences were more likely to trace, that is, 43 per cent of those with adverse factors as opposed to 23 per cent of those without;

the majority of those intending to trace wished to use an intermediary and only 18 (3.5 per cent) gave counsellors cause for concern by their attitudes;

court responses varied considerably: adoption agencies, where involved, were best able to help with information;

adoptive parents were not usually aware of the application: applicants feared misunderstanding of their application and were markedly loyal to their adoptive parents;

applicants endorsed more openness in adoption and hoped for less secrecy and stigma as a result of the legislation. Some expressed the hope that a central register could be set up to enable birth parents and other relatives to record vital information and wishes regarding tracing.

A third piece of research was commissioned by the Department of Health and Social Security, under the direction of Professor Noel Timms at the University of Newcastle-upon-Tyne.[45] This large-scale survey looked at how local authorities set up their procedures. The researchers also interviewed a number of counsellors, and 45 adopted people who sought access to their records. As in the other studies, no evidence emerged to suggest that adopted people were abusing the facility of access to information. On the contrary, there was evidence to suggest that they were giving careful consideration to the possible consequences of their actions. One counsellor commented: 'It always amazes me how sensible people are.' Both researchers and adopted people endorsed the role of social workers as counsellors but drew attention to the lack of systematic discussion about this in Parliament.

Haimes and Timms claim to have identified three counselling strategies: 'the enabler, the detective and the safeguarder'. The enabler and the detective are part of the same continuum, the latter being more active, where the counsellor is essentially satisfied about the understanding, motivation and likely conduct of the adopted person. The 'safeguarder' strategy is employed when the counsellor is concerned about the adopted person. While the employment of the latter strategy might seem legitimate in some circumstances, it does beg questions about the subjective views of some counsellors, questions which were perhaps echoed in our own research where some adopted people felt that strong unspoken messages were being conveyed, even by social workers, to leave well alone. The fact that in the Haimes and Timms study almost a quarter of the original sample of adopters was eliminated by counsellors on the subjective judgement that they were 'mentally unstable' must cast some doubt upon some of the inferences and conclusions drawn from the research. Their findings that no serious problems emerged perhaps pose more questions than they answer about counselling. It is worrying that there is an apparent suggestion that adopted people, at such a stressful and vulnerable time in their lives, should not require therapeutic help. There seemed to be some confusion about the counselling role in the minds both of researchers and of counsellors. The researchers seemed to have a theoretical perspective which could not admit that adopted people could possibly want anything other than information. They felt that unwanted counselling was 'forced' upon them. Counsellors, on the other hand, may have been discomfited as a result of working with people without obvious and immediately accessible problems and with sophisticated and subtle defence and communication systems. It is of course important to be clear about the counselling role and to have a clear contract with the adopted person, and in our view indefensible to withhold any information to which they might have a right. Despite the lack of clarity about the counselling role in Parliament, the allocation of this role to social workers with the implied recognition of certain skills and methodology, plus the comments in the introductory circular,[46] in our view carry a clear implication of help for adopted people and not simply concern for the potential problems for birth parents, as has been argued by Haimes and Timms.

In the First Report to Parliament on the Children Act 1975, made in November 1979, it is estimated that between one and two per cent of those eligible have made application under Section 26, rather fewer than anticipated. The numbers of applications received from 26 November 1976 to 31 December 1978 were as follows:

Year	Applications	Total counselled		
		M	F	Total
1976	1,991	120	234	354
(26.11–31.12)		(34%)	(66%)	
1977	3,458	1,333	3,007	4,340
		(31%)	(69%)	
1978	2,220	596	1,290	1,886
		(32%)	(68%)	

Source: Table E, page 49, First Report to Parliament on Children Act 1975.

The report states that approximately 90 per cent of those counselled intended to obtain their birth certificates, 70 per cent intended to seek information from courts, and approximately 40 per cent intended to trace their birth parents. It also notes that no significant difference was recorded between the intentions expressed by men and women.

The remarkable drop in numbers from 3,458 in 1977 to 2,220 in 1976 is probably explained by the intense publicity immediately before, during and after the implementation of the legislation, and the 'backlog' of people who had been waiting for this opportunity. Leeding commented that, in the period of his study in the West Midlands area, the referral rate was approximately 51 for every million of the population; in Cornwall, Gloucestershire and Avon it was approximately 70 per million of the population. Based upon national statistics he estimated that in July 1977, after eight months of the operation of the procedure, the rate was about 100 per million population. However, there was clearly a significant drop in 1978 and it would be unwise to attempt to predict likely future trends based upon the rather slender and extremely fluctuating date. Since 1978 numbers have increased, as follows:

Period	Applications	Counselled
1979	1,375	1,075
1980	1,547	1,412
1981	2,247	1,754
1982	2,277	1,684
1983	2,745	2,216

Later developments
An interesting development directly related to the implementation of section 26 was the establishment in 1982 of the National Organisation for Reunion of Child and Parent, known as NORCAP. Significantly, the organisation now uses the same initials for the title National Organisation for Counselling Adoptees and their Parents. This organisation seeks to provide a counselling and support service to adults involved in adoption, including a national adoption contact register and an intermediary service.

More recently, and also of significance to the discussion about formation of identity and the right to 'know who you are', has been the establishment of the Child Migrant Trust in 1987. The trust developed out of an informal post-adoption group set up by a Nottinghamshire social worker, Margaret Humphries. The group led to contact with cases of children in the care of the major voluntary child care organisations and the churches between 1870 and 1967, who were transported to the colonies to meet the need for 'British stock' and for labour. In *Lost children of the empire*[47] there are moving descriptions of the plight of these children, most of whom were not orphans and many of whom had no idea of what was happening to them. The compelling message is of the incomplete sense of identity which blights even those individuals coping satisfactorily with life in general. For many of the 1500 cases thus far referred to the Child Migrant Trust it is only now that psychological 'wholeness' has become a possibility.

The information derived both from surveys of the implementation of Section 26 and from the experience of the above organisations should help to inform practice.

The study we describe in the following chapter took place at a similar period but is different in scale from the large surveys described earlier. It examines a relatively small group in rather more depth, and it was initiated after the counselling process was completed. It had the added advantage, as do the McWhinnie[48] and Triseliotis[49] studies, of consistency of approach of one interviewer. It provides both useful confirmations of, and interesting differences from, earlier studies.

References

1 'Children Act 1975: Implementation of section 26, access by adopted people to birth records' DHSS circular no 164/76, 1976.

2 Rowe J 'The realities of adoptive parenthood' *Child adoption* 59, 1970.

3 Kornitzer M *The Holywell family* and *Mr Fairweather and his family* Bodley Head, 1960.

Rowe J *Yours by choice* Routledge & Kegan Paul, 1982.

Kornitzer M 'The adopted adolescent and the sense of identity' *Child adoption* 66, 1971.

Explaining adoption, a guide for adoptive parents ABAA, 1972.

Stevenson O *Someone else's child* Routledge & Kegan Paul, 1977.

4 Tucker T F *A guide to adoption practice* HMSO, 1970.

5 Cooper J D *Patterns of family placement – current issues in adoption and fostering* National Children's Bureau, 1978.

6 Donley K *Opening new doors* ABAFA, 1975.

7 Grow L and Shapiro D *Black children, white parents* New York: Child Welfare League of America, 1974.

8 Fanshel D *Far from the reservation* New York: Scarecrow Press, 1972.

9 Kadushin A *Adopting older children* New York: Columbia University Press, 1970.

10 Sants H J 'Genealogical bewilderment in children with substitute parents' *Brit J Med Psychol* 37, 1967.

11 Triseliotis J 'Identity and adoption' *Child adoption* 78, 1974.

12 Kornitzer M 'The adopted adolescent and the sense of identity' *Child adoption* 65, 1971.

13 McWhinnie A 'Who am I? *Child adoption* 62, 1970.

14 See 11 above.

15 See 2 above.

16 Kirk H *Shared fate* Free Press, 1964.

17 See 11 above.

18 Rosner G *Crisis of self doubt* New York: Child Welfare League of America, 1961.

19 de Hartog J *The children* Hamish Hamilton, 1969.

20 Triseliotis J *In search of origins* Routledge & Kegan Paul, 1973.

21 Erikson E H *Childhood and society* New York: W H Norton, 1950.

22 See 11 above.

23 See 12 above.

24 Kadushin A 'Reversibility of trauma' *Social work* 12 4, 1967.

25 See 11 above.

26 See 10 above.

27 Children Act 1975, section 26.

28 Report of the committee on child adoption (Cmnd 1254) HMSO, 1921.

29 Child adoption committee: First report (Cmnd 2401) HMSO, 1925;
Second report (Cmnd 2469) HMSO, 1926;
Third report (Cmnd 2711) HMSO, 1926.

30 Report of the departmental committee on the adoption of children (Cmnd 9248) HMSO, 1954.

31 Bowlby J *Attachment and loss* Hogarth Press, 1969.

32 Pringle, MLK *Adoption – facts and fallacies* Longman, 1967.

33 Rowe J *Parents, children and adoption* Routledge & Kegan Paul, 1966.

34 McWhinnie A *Adopted children, how they grow up* Routledge & Kegan Paul, 1966.

35 Report of the departmental committee on the adoption of children (Houghton Report) (Cmnd 5107) HMSO, 1972.

36 'Adoption of children: working paper containing provisional proposals by the departmental committee on the adoption of children' HMSO, 1970.

37 See 20 above.

38 Comments of members on the working paper 'Adoption of children' ABAA, 1971.

39 See 35 above.

40 Seglow J, Pringle MLK and Wedge P *Growing up adopted* NFER, 1972.

41 Members of the Standing Committee:
   Richard Crawshaw (Chair); Andrew F Bennell (Stockport N); Andrew Bowden (Brighton, Kemptown); Robert J Bradford (Belfast South); Lynda Chalker (Wallasey); Stanley Cohen (Lees, South East); Lord James Douglas Hamilton (Edinburgh, West); Norman Fowler (Sutton Coldfield); Helene Hayman (Welwyn & Hatfield); Peter Hardy (Rother Valley); Emlyn Hooson (Montgomery); Robert Hughes (Under Secretary of State for Scotland); Margaret Jackson (Lincoln); Jill Knight (Birmingham, Edgbaston); Spencer Le Merchant (High Peak); Jim Lester (Beeston); Michael Meacher (Under Secretary of State for DHSS); Millie Miller (Ilford N); Eric Moonman (Basildon); Dr David Owen (Minister of State for DHSS); Roger Sims (Bromley, Chislehurst); A W Stallard (St Pancras N); Anthony Steen (Liverpool, Lowestoft); James Tinn (Redcar); Dr Gerald Vaughan (Reading S); David Weitzman (Hackney N and Stoke Newington); Philip Whitehead (Derby N).

42 See 1 above.

43 Leeding, A 'Access to birth records' *Adoption & fostering* 1 3, 1977.

44 Social services for children in England and Wales 1976–78: Children Act 1975. First report to Parliament 1979.

45 Haimes E and Timms N *Adoption, identity and social policy* Gower, 1985.

46 See 1 above.

47 Bean P and Melville J *Lost children of the empire* Unwin Hyman, 1988.

48 See 34 above.

49 See 20 above.

3 Our research on access to records

In the previous chapter we referred to the important surveys prompted by changes in legislation. The study described here was smaller in scale but has advantages of depth. It also benefited from a series of discussions conducted with some of the respondents after the completion of the research phase. We will therefore describe it in three parts: the research, the follow-up discussions and the suggested implications for practice.

The research
The study had the purpose of recording and analysing the experiences of adopted people who chose to obtain information about themselves, with particular reference to establishing their personal and social identity. It was of course anticipated that this study would also help to inform current and future professional practice and this aspect has been pursued since through discussions with colleagues, students and others.

Methodology will not be discussed in detail here but some of the considerations were how to obtain a representative sample and how to elicit, record and analyse information. The latter question was the most demanding, as it required achieving a balance between accurate and objective recording of factual information and sensitive expression of intense and complex perceptions of human experience and feeling. It was necessary to create an environment in which respondents would feel able to share such personal information, and for the style of the interview to reflect the nature of the material to be gathered, much of which would be emotionally laden and would demand a patient, comprehensive and penetrative approach.

The most appropriate research tools were felt to be a flexibly-structured interview schedule and a rating type of questionnaire which would help to explore in a systematic way issues generally held to be relevant to the success of adoption. It was also helpful to corroborate parts of the interview, so case files, where available, were studied after interviews were completed. In some cases these yielded a great deal of additional insight into the experiences and feelings of the main protagonists at the time of the adoption.

Two other social services departments turned down the opportunity to mount the project. One refused on the grounds that staff time could not be made available to the project, the other on the basis of serious reservations of senior staff who expressed a 'fundamental anxiety' about the nature of the project and the effect it could have on adopted people. It was felt that the project could open or reopen 'areas of unresolved feelings without the availability of skilled help to deal with them'. There is clearly still a strong body of opinion which feels that such things are best left alone. Given that adopted people themselves are such a small minority of the population, however, the importance of giving their views expression assumes even greater significance. At the time the reasons for going ahead took careful account of the potential for conflict between the research task and the therapeutic needs of respondents. The following points were felt to outweigh that possibility:

potential respondents would be mature adults with freedom of choice about participation in the project. They should have the right to make that choice for themselves and not have agencies make the choice without their knowledge;

the purpose and focus of the interviews would be clearly explained in writing (in an initial letter) and verbally (at the commencement of the interview);

the interviews would not be carried out while counselling was in progress so therapeutic needs should have been already recognised and responded to;

the interviewer was a trained social worker, experienced in adoption work and in individual counselling, who would recognise therapeutic needs and respond to them appropriately within the context of the research 'contract'. The interviewer would also incorporate into the research an arrangement to re-introduce the respondent to the social worker where necessary;

the research objective and the therapeutic quality of an interview are not necessarily incompatible, indeed Bowlby[1] has claimed that to arrive at relevant data in research an interview must be potentially therapeutic;

there is considerable evidence demonstrating that, as Wolins[2] suggests, 'the client is neither so frail nor so puny as the professional tends to think him'. See, for example, Levy,[3] Maas and Polansky,[4] Kogan et al[5] and Mitchell and Mudd;[6]

finally, it was felt that account should be taken of the continuing need to refine and expand the knowledge available to practitioners. As Macdonald has stated, 'the function of social work research is to contribute to the development of a dependable body of knowledge to serve the goals and means of social work in all its ramifications.'[7] This point was felt to be particularly important as a hitherto largely-untapped source of information was becoming available.

It was also decided to omit from the sample any potential respondents with serious symptoms of formal mental illness (in consultation with the social workers/counsellors); and to ensure that social workers/counsellors were fully aware of the research and prepared to liaise with the interviewer over making contact with the sample and resuming counselling if necessary.

The study was concentrated in one county council administrative area in south-east Wales, comprising one city and smaller urban and rural areas, with widely varying cultural patterns and a consistently high level of children requiring substitute care. It was decided to contact all those referred by the General Register Office for counselling in that area from the implementation of the relevant legislation, ie 26 November 1976, until 31 December 1978. Fifty-four adopted people fell into this category.

Those 54 individuals formed the target group for the study, and were approached during 1979 and 1980. Three had moved house and could not be located and of the remaining 51, 34 agreed to participate in the study. Subsequently one respondent could not be contacted despite several attempts. However, this was an encouraging response rate of 64.7 per cent. It comprised nine males aged between 22 and 43 years and 24 females aged between 20 and 52 years (27.3 per cent male and 72.7 per cent female). The ratio of males to females in the target group, the response group and in national statistics were remarkably similar and the sample was therefore felt to typify the national picture.

A detailed examination of agency records on all those in the target group did not reveal any significant differences between respondents and non-respondents in the target group. This analysis took into account all recorded factors including adoption experiences, stated motivation and objectives in seeking biographical information, age, sex and social status. Whether the target group was representative of adopted adults in the community in general cannot be considered, in the absence of a control group, which was not available. It is possible that adopted people who did not seek access to their birth records could have been told more by their adopters.

The nature of the study was mainly descriptive but where the data obtained is capable of simple numerical presentation and analysis, it is summarised below in the form of tables and brief comment.

Table 1

Age and sex of respondents

	18–25	26–30	31–35	36–40	41–45	46–50	51–55	Total
M	3	0	5	0	1	0	0	9
F	5	4	7	5	1	1	1	24
Total	8	4	12	5	2	1	1	33

At the time of the research 30 respondents were married (seven male and 23 female); the two unmarried males were aged 21 and 22. The one unmarried female had been divorced and not remarried, while three other females had divorced and remarried. All except two of the married respondents had children of their own, and those two had adopted children.

Table 2 reveals that 28 of the respondents were married by the time they were 25, and 14 were married by the age of 20. Of the latter, ten explicitly associated their early and, in some cases, disastrous marriages with unhappiness in their adoptive home. For some it was said to be a direct result of finding out in older adolescence that they were adopted.

Of these marriages four ended in divorce, one was found to have been contracted bigamously, and two were contracted following pre-marital pregnancy. Included in these figures is a female who left home aged

Table 2

Marital status of respondents

	Age at time of first marriage				
	16–20	21–25	26–30	31–35	Total
M	1	6	0	0	7
F	13	8	2	1	24
Total	14	14	2	1	31

18 to form an apparently unstable cohabitation, and who subsequently married someone else.

Of the four divorced females, three appeared to have made stable, happy and supportive second marriages; the fourth had not remarried, was content with her situation, and had good relationships with her three adolescent children.

At the time of the interviews, the group of respondents projected a general impression of successful and satisfying marital and family relationships. In only two cases were there indications that there might be some marital disharmony.

Table 3

Living accommodation of respondents

	Owner-occupier	Rent (private)	Rent (council)	Employer-provided	Total
M	3	2	3	1	9
F	18	1	4	1	24
Total	21	3	7	2	33

All the respondents lived with their families in their own accommodation, the majority being owner-occupiers of semi-detached houses. One lived in a detached house and three in terraced houses. Eleven lived in rented accommodation provided by the local authority or private sector, and two in housing provided by employers: a special school and the Royal Air Force.

Within the limitations of these rather crude yardsticks, it would appear that the group of respondents were socially, emotionally and economically successful. With the exception of the two unmarried males, each respondent was part of an effective family unit able to provide for the physical and emotional needs of its members. All seemed occupationally successful relative to opportunity and apparent ability, and played a positive part in wider social networks of extended families and neighbourhoods.

The two unmarried males were in regular employment and one, who was about to embark upon a degree course, appeared to have a substantial number of satisfying personal relationships. There was evidence that the other had some difficulty in making and sustaining personal relationships.

It would seem reasonable to conclude that the data provided by this group of respondents is unlikely to be distorted by abnormalities of personality or any excessive pressures generated by their current situations. On the contrary, they present as a mature group, probably fairly typical of the adult population, and their experiences, opinions and attitudes are felt to be of great significance to theory and practice.

Adoption data
One of the objectives of this study was to examine the adoption experience of respondents and here, too, much of the data is quantifiable.

Table 4

Year in which adoption order made

	1930/ 1935	1936/ 1940	1941/ 1945	1945/ 1950	1951/ 1955	1956/ 1960	Total
M	1	0	1	4	0	3	9
F	2	1	9	3	5	4	24
Total	3	1	10	7	5	7	33

Adoption orders in respect of the respondents were made between the years 1931 and 1960 with a peak during and immediately after the war years 1941–1945. This reflects the national adoption statistical trends.

63

Twelve orders were made in the county courts, 20 in magistrates' courts and one in the Chancery Division of the High Court.

Table 5

Age of child at time of order

	4–6 months	7–12 months	13–18 months	19–24 months	2–3 years	3–4 years	4–5 years	Total
M	3	2	2	0	2	0	0	9
F	12	7	1	1	2	0	1	24
Total	15	9	3	1	4	0	1	33

The ages of children at the time of their adoption varied between four months and four years six months; 24 were adopted before they were six months old. Those adopted in their second year or later tended to be either intra-family adoptions (two); children born of an extramarital relationship (one); or children who were for a period in the care of the local authority (two).

Table 6

Arrangements for adoption placement

	Adoption agency	Local authority	3rd party/ direct	Total
M	2	5	2	9
F	9	8	7	24
Total	11	13	9	33

Placement arrangements varied, 24 being made by adoption agencies or a local authority, and nine by third parties or direct by the child's mother.

Thirty of the respondents (23 male and seven female) were born to single unmarried parents, while three (two male and one female) said they had been born of their mother's extra-marital relationship. The latter group had either been rejected by their mother's husband, or had been secretly placed for adoption without their mother's husband being aware of their existence.

Table 7

Age of adoptive mothers at time of adoption

	21–25	26–30	31–35	36–40	41–45	46–50	51–55	56–60	Total
M	1	0	2	2	1	1	0	1	8
F	1	2	10	5	4	2	0	0	24
Total	2	2	12	7	5	3	0	1	32

(*NB No information is available on one set of parents*)

Table 8

Age of adoptive fathers at time of adoption

	21–25	26–30	31–35	36–40	41–45	46–50	51–55	56–60	Total
M	0	3	0	2	1	1	1	0	8
F	0	1	11	5	5	2	0	0	24
Total	0	4	11	7	6	3	1	0	32

(*NB No information is available on one set of parents*)

Being told
Being told, or finding out, that one is adopted is inevitably a very significant event, and all the respondents could clearly remember how this occurred.

Table 9

Respondents who were voluntarily told of their adoption by parents (by age)

	0–5	6–10	11–15	16–20	Over 21	Total
M	3	2	0	0	0	5
F	5	4	1	0	0	10
Total	8	6	1	0	0	15

Fewer than half of the respondents were told about their adoption voluntarily by their parents. Of these, eight felt that they had 'always known', and all had been told by the age of 12 years. These adoptions where 'telling' had occurred voluntarily were representative of the three types of placement arrangements: adoption agency placements (six), local authority placements (four) and thier prty or direct placements (five).

Without exception, those respondents who had been told of their adoption by their parents had been given negligible information, and all except one had found it quite impossible to have further discussions about it with their parents. Some had made occasional attempts to discuss their origins further but their overwhelming memories were of the pain and discomfort of their adoptive parents and of their own feelings of shame, uncertainty and guilt about hurting them.

One man could clearly recall being told of his adoption by his mother at the age of four or five. He happened to be looking in the mirror at the time and was insistent that it was not 'this Johnny' but 'that Johnny', his mirror image, about whom his mother was talking.

A young women who did feel able to discuss her adoption with her parents, or more specifically her mother, had grown up with the knowledge of her adoption and at the age of 13 was given all the relevant papers to keep in her bedroom. Her experience was unique among the respondents in that she could raise the subject easily and discussions were relaxed; unfortunately, however, her mother had only minimal information and she found this very frustrating. She had a turbulent adolescence, became pregnant before marriage and married at the age of 17. However, she has a stable marriage and a very good relationship with her widowed adoptive mother. Significantly, she was one of only two respondents who had been able to tell their adoptive parents of their intention to seek out their birth records. She remained highly motivated to obtain information about her origins.

The remaining 18 respondents, that is 56 per cent of the total, were told of their adoption by others, found out by discovering documents or, having had their suspicions aroused, challenged their parents or others. the youngest of this group was aged five and the oldest 35.

For six of these respondents the critical time came when birth certificates had to be presented at school. For some, this was at the age of six or seven and for others at ten or 11. In most cases adoptive parents, usually mothers, responded with confusion and often insisted

Table 10

Respondents who found out about their adoption (by age)					
	0–5	6–10	11–15	16–20	Over 21	Total
M	0	2	2	0	0	4
F	1	4	5	2	2	14
Total	1	6	7	2	2	18

upon taking the certificate to the school themselves, still not telling the child of the adoption. This inevitably led to suspicion and eventually challenge from the child. For some children the demand for the birth certificate produced a hasty, embarrassed explanation of the adoption; one respondent recalled being told of her adoption for the first time in the school lunch hour.

Five of the respondents were told by other children in various situations, frequently in the form of taunts following fights and arguments. One man recalled having a fight with another boy at the age of 11 and being taunted with the fact that he was adopted. He ran home crying to his mother who confirmed the fact but offered no explanation saying that he would be told when he was old enough. That night he temporarily ran away from home and subsequently felt resentful towards his parents and an 'outsider' in the family. He was never given further information and at the age of 42, despite being happily married and highly successful in his work, he was still deeply troubled by his lack of knowledge of himself and quite unable to talk to his mother about his origins and adoption.

Two respondents had the difficult experience of finding out about their adoption from individuals operating in a professional role. In one case a 17-year old girl, visiting her practitioner with whom she had been registered for many years, was called by a name she did not recognise and when she questioned this, was told that the name was written on her records. She was already concerned about some conflicting information she had been given by her parents, although she had not suspected that she might be adopted. Being called by another name, made her think about the possibility of adoption but when challenged, her parents totally denied that she was adopted.

A boy of eight found out after his teacher at school asked those who were adopted to hold their hands up. He did not know what the word meant and went home and asked his mother. His experience was more positive because his mother, although upset, was prepared to talk at length with him about his adoption. He recalls further discussion at the age of 13 prompted by the insistence of the local vicar that his parents should talk to him about his adoption before he was confirmed as a member of the church.

Two extreme examples of not being told by their adoptive parents concerned two older women. One, aged 35, was told by her husband after the death of her parents. The other, aged 28, was told by an ex-neighbour she happened to meet whom she had not seen for some years. The former said that she had been shocked but felt no bitterness and could perfectly understand the protective motivation of her parents. The latter said that she was 'shattered' and wandered about for hours in a dazed condition.

One of the most interesting facts to emerge from this data is that those respondents who were voluntarily told of their adoption by their parents did not necessarily feel better about their situation than those who were not told. The crucial elements appear to be the amount and the accuracy of the information available, the ability of the adoptive parents to recognise and share in the feelings of the adopted child about the adoption, and particularly their appreciation of the child's need to explore the question 'Who am I?'. The experiences and feelings of respondents in both groups were markedly similar.

No respondents had recieved any meaningful information about their origins; many spoke of extreme tensions and even taboo preventing any discussion of adoption; all had feelings ranging from discomfort in their difference from others, and anger about not having information to which they felt entitled, to guilt about causing distress to their adoptive parents. The majority felt stigmatised by their adoptive state. In terms of Goffman's[8] description of the three main types of stigma, this feeling would derive from 'abominations of the body' and 'blemishes of individual character', the first a subtle product of common attitudes towards childlessness (traditionally the main motivation to adoption), the second a more obvious, and for the respondents more potent, reaction to illegitimacy.

Access to birth records
Respondents were questioned about their intensions and objectives in

seeking access to their birth records and predictably the main motivation was the quest for self-identity through biographical information and meeting blood relatives. The most common trigger experiences were the birth of a baby, the need for family medical histories, and the death of adoptive parents. All the respondents who were parents spoke very movingly of the joy and wonder of having someone of their 'own flesh and blood'. The publicity surrounding the change in adoption law was of course itself also a trigger.

A few respondents were clear from the outset that they wished to pursue their origins as far as they could, including meeting their birth parents, provided this was consistent with not being destructive to them.

One respondent was firm in his intention simply to find out where she was born. She had three children and was pregnant for the fourth time when interviewed. In the town where she lived, a continuing research project which had been conducted over many previous years, was recording data on all babies born in the area. She had never been able to answer the researcher's question about where she herself had been born and felt this gap in her knowledge keenly. She derived enormous pleasure from the knowledge that during her next confinement she would be able to answer that question. There was, however, some indication subsequently that, despite her firm protestations at that time, she was considering making further investigations into her origins.

The majority of respondents were less clear and confident regarding their intentions, and much seemed to depend upon the practical help and advice available and the explicit and implicit santions applied by those around them. Practical difficulties also seriously affected progress. For example, travelling to London to search in the General Registered Office or visiting areas with early associations, was a daunting prospect for young mothers with children or those without transport. The problem was compounded for many by the need for secrecy and the consequent difficulty of explaining absence. Female respondents in particular felt guilty about using what they perceived as family time, finance and transport for such a self-indulgent activity.

Some respondents felt unable to fathom the intricacies of record systems alone, and several were reluctant to approach agencies for information in their records. Some were told that records had been destroyed or, in the case of courts, could not be found or would not be made available. It is easy to understand the enormous frustration which built up in respondents who felt at times, with apparently some justification, that agencies and individuals were unhelpful and that attitudes to the storage of personal records were unsatisfactory, infinitely variable and occasionally even cavalier. Of the respondents whose placements were arranged by agencies, some had large detailed personal dossiers even including lists of clothing they had when leaving their birth mothers. Some, of course, had files with very basic and erratic recording and others, including some of the youngest respondents, two of whom were placed by the same agency in the West Midlands, were told that the agency had closed and their records had been destroyed. Where files existed, their use and accessibility was unpredictable and inconsistent.

One respondent was allowed to read through his file in the company of the social worker, others were allowed selected access to documents in an attempt to preserve confidential recording about other parties, and a few were actually given copies of letters or other interesting documents: one man was even given what appeared to be the only file copy of a guardian *ad litem* report. One woman poignantly described her experience of visiting the London headquarters of a national adoption society and her acute frustration at watching the agency representative slowly turn the pages of a thick file, which she could see contained several letters from both her parents, while waiting for the crumbs of selected information she was to be given.

Table 11 shows a summary of contacts made by respondents at the time of the initial research. We know that at a later stage several took their actions further and we cannot stress too strongly how much this depended upon the attitudes of family and friends. The group discussion described later certainly led to further action by some of the respondents.

All except one male and one female respondent obtained their original birth certificate (column A). The man was motivated partly by the fact that his baby son was due to have a whooping cough vaccination and, following questions asked at the clinic, his wife was anxious about possible inheritable medical contra-indications. The woman had obtained information on her place of birth, which was all she initially wanted. However, she was later seriously considering obtaining her birth certificate.

Columns B to N in the table reflect a variety of actions by the same

Table 11

Summary of contact made by respondents in their search

	A	B	C	D	E	F	G	H	I	J	K	L	M	N
M	8	3	2	5	0	0	0	3	3	0	2	0	1	1
F	23	6	9	6	1	3	1	3	3	3	3	3	1	1
Total	31	9	11	11	1	3	1	6	6	3	5	3	2	2

Key:
A – Obtain birth certificate   B – Contact court
C – Contact agency   D – Visit area of origin
E – Advertise (press)   F – Contact Salvation Army
G – Employ genealogist   H – Visit General Register Office
I – Meet mother   J – Meet father
K – Meet family   L – Write mother
M – Write father   N – Contact parent(s) via social worker

individuals, each column indicating how may respondents undertook that particular action.

The highest levels of activity were associated with contacting the agency which had arranged the adoption and visiting the area of origin and place of birth. As indicated, earlier records available in agencies varied considerably as did the approach of the agency representatives or the counselling social workers involved. In some instances, respondents themselves visited the agencies concerned and in other the counselling social worker obtained the relevant records on loan. Three respondents approached the Salvation Army missing persons service for assistance but were informed that it was not their policy to become involved in these circumstances. One respondent advertised in local newspapers giving her original name and present age, and asking anyone who knew her to get in contact. This effort unfortunately only produced a few responses from individuals hoping to lay claim to a legacy, but no bona fide relatives or friends.

Visits to St Catherine's House to search records yielded varying degress of success relative to informaiton already available, a degree of luck and the abilities and tenancity of the respondents. One, who had earlier in his career beeen employed by a finance company to trace debtors, demonstrated that it was easy to trace other people provided that one 'knows the ropes'. Clearly the organisation, approach, intelligence, support and sheer stamina of the respondents were critical factors.

Six respondents eventually succeeded in meeting their mothers, three in meeting their fathers, and five met other members of their families such as half-siblings, aunts, uncles and grandparents. (We know that these numbers increased substantially months, and even years, after the research was completed.) A further three corresponded with their mothers. One planned to go on to meet her mother, one was unsure, and in the third case the mother was unwilling to meet her.

Two corresponded with their fathers, one eventually traced her father who had emigrated to Australia and they subsequently corresponded. One respondent, having traced his father, wrote two letters to him, the first brief and factual and handed over by the social worker explaining that he had also written a much longer, detailed letter. The second letter had photographs of himself and his wife and children and was left with the social worker to be given to his father should he wish it. In this case, the father wanted no further contact and that letter is still on file in the social services department.

Another letter, from a female respondent, written after her mother refused to meet her, demonstrates clearly the motivation and desire of many of the respondents:

> ... Mrs L (the social worker who has been helping me find out facts about myself) rang me approximately one hour ago [to tell me you did not wish to have contact] ... I naturally will not worry you any further and felt I had to put your mind at rest on that point. But I felt also that I had to make my motives in finding you clear. My parents love me very much and I them, so I can assure you that I wasn't looking for 'mother love', I have an abundance of that already. I wanted to know about myself especially since the birth of my children. My son looks very much like my husband. My daughter looks like me, and perhaps you, one can never tell. I wanted to know who I looked like, at what time I was born, how heavy I was, stupid ordinary facts most people take for granted. I wanted to know what you looked like too.
>
> I am sure that there must be dogs on your farm that have a longer pedigree than mine. I know one of our dogs has.

I didn't want to form a long lasting relationship with you, I just wanted to meet you, just once . . .

Many of the respondents indicated the significance to them of the nature of the birth parents' relationship. The frequent comment made was: 'I'm glad it wasn't a one night stand', and pleasure was always expressed at information indicating a more than superficial relationship between parents. Most respondents were conscious of their illegitimacy and sensitive to the attitudes of others, male respondents in particular talking of responding aggressively to the word 'bastard'. The general sensitivity to illegitimacy was even more apparent in the discussion group set up following the research when, at a very early stage, a member of the group commented: 'We're all illegitimate here then.' This remark was greeted with relief, laughter and a tremendous sense of understanding and identification within the group.

Counselling
In the social services department concerned in this research, counselling was carried out by a small group of social workers specialising in fostering and adoption work. As this group had also received in-service training prior to the implementation of Section 26 of the Children Act 1975, a relatively high level of quality of counselling could be assumed.

With the exception of the one respondent who did not take up appointments offered, all the respondents had received counselling by virtue of the fact that they were adopted before 28 November 1976. On average each received approximately two hours interview time. The minimum contact was one interview of approximately 45 minutes, and the maximum contact was seven interviews, one with a social worker from another local authority. All the respondents confirmed that they had been offered further counselling time to be provided at their request. However, only nine respondents had more than one interview, and the subsequent interviews appeared to be associated with a tangible focus such as obtaining further information, or the social worker acting as an intermediary.

The respondents appeared to like their social workers and generally agreed that the idea behind counselling was sound, although some said that they had initially resented having to see a social worker before they could obtain information to which they felt they had a right. One respondent said that the idea of seeing a social worker was more frightening at first than the idea of seeking out her origins.

When asked about the helpfulness of counselling, six respondents were enthusiastically positive, 13 were disappointed or even felt it was a waste of time, and another 13 found it quite helpful. To some extent, perceptions of the usefulness of counselling were related to the success of the applicant in achieving his or her objectives, and one respondent who talked about 'red tape' and long intervals between interviews had, according to the social worker's record, frequently failed to keep appointments.

Some implications of the research

This study, like others before it, is diminished by the lack of a control group of those who decided not to seek access to their birth records. Nationally, the proportion of those taking advantage of the change in the law was one to two per cent. Earlier it was demonstrated that the respondents seemed typical of the target group, but how representative the target group was of adopted adults in the community cannot be demonstrated conclusively. However, the published findings of Raynor's large-scale study[9] would suggest that the respondents were fairly typical. (This study involved all adopted adults placed between 1948 and 1951 by the Thomas Coram Foundation.)

The proportions of males to females, the periods during which orders were made and the ages of respondents are broadly similar to those in other studies, for example, Leeding[10] Triseliotis[11] and Day.[12]

Respondents were generally felt to be stable, reasonably well-adjusted individuals, concerned about and sensitive to the position and feelings of their birth and adoptive parents. Their primary allegiance was to those who had actually carried out the parenting role. There were no examples in the study of irresponsible and damaging behaviour by respondents, despite the use of a number of unusual and enterprising strategies. This confirms other findings and suggests that the fears expressed in 1976, often in extreme and hysterical parlance,* were largely groundless.

---

*For example, News of the World, 10 October 1976: 'Mums in fear of knock at the door'; Daily Mirror, 11 October 1976: Haunted by the past'; Daily Telegraph, 11 October 1976: 'Fear of emotional upsets over "reveal-all" adoption law'.

The possibility of distortion arising from the self-selection of the respondents must, of course, be recognised. The Triseliotis study recorded that the majority of those seeking genealogical information and contact with birth parents tended to be 'unhappy and lonely people'. Our study did not support that finding, and neither did that of Timms and Haimes.[13] We can only conclude that there is still no definitive answer to the question of why some adoptees seek information and some do not. It seems likely that those with a bad experience of adoption, or who have been given little information, will be highly motivated to investigate their background. However, it is a reasonable assumption that the vast majority of adopted people were given very little information simply because their adopters never had it, or because for them it was insignificant compared with the emotional intensity of their own early experience of parenthood, and was repressed or forgotten. It also seems possible that guilt or fear of disapproval would prevent adopted people from seeking information at least as much as apathy or total satisfaction with their lot.

A further question which might be posed about our findings is that of their relevance to present-day practice. We feel that while there have been undoubted developments in related theory, and small pockets of excellence in practice, there is no evidence on a comprehensive scale that adoption practice has improved significantly. In fact, the general broadening of social workers' tasks since genericism was established through the Local Authority Social Services Act in 1970, coupled with the reduction in the number of adoptions throughout the 1970s, could suggest dissipation and decline in knowledge and skills in the field of adoption.

In addition, the recent emphasis in teaching, research and writing upon the family placement of hard-to-place children has perhaps compounded the problems of maintaining and developing basic skills in the more conventional adoption placement of very young children.

The respondents themselves provided further evidence of relatively unchanged societal attitudes. They often commented upon aspects of their own experiences being replicated at the present time among adopted children growing up. This evidence is of course anecdotal and no conclusions may be drawn from it, but we feel it to be of some worth. The respondents were, after all, a group of well-informed people sensitive to the state of adoption. In individual interviews and in group discussions, several recounted current examples within their own family and social circles of adoptive parents unable to have open discourse with their children and telling lies and half-truths to the children and others. There were also examples of insensitivity and sheer ignorance about adoption and adopted children among school teachers, health visitors and doctors. At this time, more than 50 years after adoption became legal, it is disappointing that professionals in such sensitive positions do not display a more sophisticated under-standing.

The follow-up discussion group
It became apparent during the research interviews that many individuals felt isolated and deprived of opportunities to talk about feelings and perceptions with those who shared a common experience, despite having supportive families and spouses. This led us to suggest to each of them individually that they might appreciate an opportunity to meet with others who had sought access to their birth records. We set up an initial meeting as a one-off social gathering with the possibility of a further series of discussion meetings if participants wished. Several of the original respondents lived at some distance from the main centre of the study, and others had since moved. In the event 15 people attended this meeting and any trepidation instantly appeared to melt in what can only be described as the spontaneous eruption of long-repressed experiences and emotions. The presence of anyone other than the respondents was quite unnecessary for a substantial part of the time. The entire group quickly became relaxed in an experience which seemed at once cathartic, informative and full of good humour. The meeting concluded with the consideration of forming a discussion group to explore further some of the issues arising from the research. Eleven members made this practical commitment and met on six occasions during an eight-month period in 1981/82. These meetings were tape-recorded by consent and a clear 'contract' established. The purpose of discussions was to be a shared exchange of information and experience. Our role was to facilitate, inform or interpret where necessary, and to record, *not* to provide therapy. At the same time it was recognised that the group process could be therapeutic and mutually supportive.

What followed was for us a privileged experience. The participants were impressive in their willingness to share personal experiences, often of great pain and intensity, and in their generosity in listening to and supporting colleagues. Their honesty, enthusiasm and openness with ourselves as a potential channel for achieving improvements in understanding and practice was, to say the least, daunting.

After the series of group meetings had ended there were a few, predominantly social, contacts with the group between 1982 and 1986. Of particular interest from these contacts was the discovery that several individuals had taken their quest for information and contact much further. These developments seemed to be attributable to a variety of factors, not least the support and sometimes the practical help of other members of the group, which helped to confirm that the desire for information really was legitimate. The simple passage of time, however, which allows emotional space to absorb one experience or set of information before moving on to another, was probably an important factor, and this reinforces the dangers of reaching hasty conclusions about the motivation and objectives of adopted people who seek information. It seems likely that at the point of counselling (and therefore of much research on the subject), respondents are not only likely to be highly defensive but may also only be at the start of a long process.

On the whole the discussion group served to expand upon and illuminate, sometimes much more clearly and vividly, information gathered in the research. It seems appropriate therefore to combine discussion of the recurrent themes of these two phases and of their possible implications for practice and this is done in the next chapter.

References

1 Bowlby J *Maternal care and mental health* World Health Organisation, 1951.

2 Wolins M 'Measuring the effect of social work intervention' in Polansky N A (ed) *Social work research* University of Chicago Press, 1960.

3 Levy D 'A follow-up study of unmarried mothers' *Social casework* 35, 1955.

4 Maas H S and Polansky N A 'Collecting original data' *Social work research*, 1950.

5 Kogan L S, Hunt J McW and Bartelme P *A follow-up study of the results of social casework* New York: Family service association of America, 1953.

6 Mitchell H E and Mudd E H 'Anxieties associated with the conduct of research in a clinical setting' *Amer J Orthophychiat* 27, 1957.

7 Macdonald M E 'Social work research: a perspective' in Polansky N A (ed) *Social work research* University of Chicago Press, 1960.

8 Goffman E *Stigma: notes on the management of spoiled identity* Penguin Books, 1963.

9 Raynor L *The adopted child comes of age* Allen and Unwin, 1980.

10 Leeding A 'The local authority experience' in Hall T (ed) *Access to birth records* ABAFA, 1980.

11 Triseliotis J *In search of origins* Routledge & Kegan Paul, 1973.

12 Day C 'General register office study' in Hall T (ed) *Access to birth records* ABAFA, 1980.

13 Haimes E and Timms N *Adoption, identity and social policy* Gower, 1985.

4 Implications for practice

Not surprisingly, most of the respondents in the research study and follow-up group emphasised the same points. At a very simple level the experiences of several respondents reinforced the fundamental importance of ascertaining the adoptive parents' state of mental and physical health and the quality of their matrimonial relationship.

Telling

Predictably, most clearly highlighted were the issues surrounding telling the child of the adoption and giving biographical information. Two most interesting points arise from the research information. First, only 41 per cent of adopters in 'agency' placements voluntarily told their children, whereas 55 per cent of adopters in 'private' placements did. Second, the simple fact of 'telling' would appear to be much less important than the method and content, or than continuing open communication on the subject.

The overwhelming evidence on this point came in answers to detailed questions about the selection of adopters. Here the unanimous view of respondents was that the single most important factor was the ability to be completely open and honest with a child. Even those respondents who had been told of their adoption at an early age had been given virtually no information and, with the one exception mentioned earlier, found discussion to be impossible because of parental resistance and embarrassment, and because of their own feelings of guilt about wanting to know yet 'hurting' their parents.

Whether respondents were deprived of information because their adopters did not have any, or because they were unable to share what they knew, is unclear. Some were certainly subjected to inaccuracies and fabrications by their adopters.

These issues of open communication, of honesty and of giving full information are clearly cause for continuing concern. The willingness and ability of adopters to be completely open and honest with their adopted child is a difficult and perhaps impossible quality to assess accurately at the time of their application and approval. The answer may therefore partly rest with the availability of skilled counselling at critical times. Although the actual provision of such a service may be relatively simple, the problems of making it known, understood, and above all, acceptable to adopters and to the wider community, are much more complex.

At a simple and practical level the arguments for providing adopters with full written information about their child seem overwhelming. However, given the apparent inability of some adopters to share the information, a duplicate copy should also be retained by the agency to be made available to the adult adopted person on request. It might also be helpful if agencies were given more specific guidance regarding the type of information to be sought and retained.

The practice of telling children when they are young but without providing subsequent opportunities to reiterate and explore the meanings and implications of adoption raises a number of important questions. First, small children may become confused, even about the word itself. One respondent revealed that for quite a long time she thought it had something to do with illness; at about the same time that the word 'adopted' was introduced to her, the family cat was 'doctored'. The similarity of the two words had stuck in her mind. Second, small children do not always know enough to ask supplementary questions related to the information they are given. Later, if the parents do not open the subject up again in a secure and confident way, the child may become more uncomfortable and more likely to respond to the non-verbal signals not to ask questions. Since it is possible that some of these 'non-communications' derive from adopters' own responses to illegitimacy coupled with, perhaps, feelings associated with their own childlessness, if this applies, it would be entirely understandable if the child became aware of tension engendered by such circumstances. Such tensions and mysteries may mean to the child that there is something wrong with them, and this becomes integrated with the need to maintain secrecy into adult life.

Sometimes, regrettably, adopters told lies about the children's origins, as at least two of the respondents in our study discovered. One recalled 'knowing' as quite a young child that her mother was not really her mother and then, when trying to establish the truth of her identity as a teenager, having this denied. The extent of children's acute sensitivity to adult secrets should not come as any great surprise. Most of us can recall being aware of things as children which our parents or other adults imagined us to be ignorant of. For this woman, however, coping with adolescent uncertainty as well as the denial of a strongly suspected truth about herself, created severe distress. She described the feeling as thinking she was going mad. Eventually it was explained that her birth mother had never wanted her and had given her away when she was two days old. This was later found to be untrue. Another group member was told a similar story of a feckless and wilful mother who had eagerly disposed of her baby at the earliest opportunity. This person later discovered that not only did her mother care for her until she was about eight months old but she had carefully prepared clothes and belongings for the baby before parting with her.

Why is it that being open and honest with children about their origins is so difficult? The need for this is well established: as early as the 1950s the Hurst Committee took evidence which pointed to the damaging effects of failure to provide such information. Later practice and research has confirmed this view. The BAAF publication *Explaining adoption to your adopted child*[1] reinforces the point: 'Children who discover unexpectedly that a loved parent is not, after all, a blood relation have their faith and trust in that parent shattered.' Adopters were not included in our research, and it is perhaps too easy to be critical of them for their apparent evasiveness and lack of honesty, as they – and indeed social workers too – have little real help in preparing for the powerful emotions which can engulf honest but intellectual intentions about 'telling'.

An earlier involvement with an adoptive mother sharing her feelings with a group of prospective adopters illustrates the point well. The group had agreed that the child had a right to know, and that it was their responsibility to ensure that the child heard the truth from them. The mother said:

> I wanted him to get used to hearing the word even before he could understand it so that he would accept it as natural. So one day when he was about ten months old, I thought 'this is the day, I'll do it for the first time today, I'll tell him.' I waited until after his bath and I had him on my lap and I wanted to say to him 'you are my little adopted baby and I love you very much'. But I couldn't do it. I couldn't say the words. I just held him and I cried.

This underlines how important it is for social workers to go further than a superficial acceptance of statements of intent and belief about giving and sharing information with the child. It may not, as illustrated above, be easy, and whatever the intent the more typical pattern may be that the subject becomes taboo within the adoptive family.

At the same time, an insistence upon facing possibly distressing issues in a vacuum may be equally unhelpful. Social work skill and judgement is at a premium in such an area. It may be that all that can be done is to identify potential stress and difficulty and enter the subject on the agenda as one with which future social work help will almost certainly be needed. This at least allows room for further consideration and does not force adopters into defensive and unhappy positions. However when, or if, the reality is faced with a child, there might be a higher level of sensitivity and acceptance of help when it is really needed.

Childlessness and infertility
The most likely source of resistance to being open and honest with an adopted child will for many parents be feelings about childlessness and infertility. Fantasies and myths similar to those surrounding illegitimacy are sadly experienced by numbers of couples who wish to adopt because of an inability to produce a child of their own. The sense of failure, guilt or shame which may be experienced by many people in this situation is comprehensively and often very movingly discussed by Diane and Peter Houghton.[2]

Involuntarily childless people cannot be guaranteed a sensitive, supportive and caring response from those around them. On the contrary, they may have experienced a good deal of cruelty and censure. Some women are still told, and may still believe, despite the educative influence of the women's movement, that they are incomplete or unfulfilled unless they produce a family. A letter published in the *Independent* took issue with a view of infertility expressed in a recent article:

> I tried unsuccessfully for some time to conceive and then a more serious disease was diagnosed and I was advised, for the sake of my health and the future of any child, not to try and have a family.

> I do therefore understand the anguish which results in so much discussion on the subject...

However, I feel that the attitudes so often expressed . . . are more what I would have expected from society in Victorian England or before the last war. Women without children should not see their life ahead as empty . . . We do not need children to be accepted by society . . .

I would say to those who cannot have children, stop worrying about what you cannot have and start to enjoy the benefits and advantages that are open to you.[3]

The fact that the writer felt compelled to express herself so strongly suggests that she has experienced some of those traditional values and attitudes which continue to haunt us despite more than a decade of social liberation: this is a further illustration of the effect of stigma as described by Goffman.[4] Childless men too are not spared distress, becoming a butt of cruel or ribald 'jokes' concerning their sexual prowess or their innate masculinity.

Married couples without children may be treated with pity or indeed with hostility or envy.

For a couple trying to conceive or undergoing fertility tests or treatment which can often be quite distressing, such attitudes must be very hard to bear. Many childless couples who want to start a family often choose to keep quiet, concealing the truth from all but the very closest of family and friends.

Clearly, any attempt to present a definitive or generally applicable explanation for attitudes to childlessness will be spurious. Nevertheless, a core of complex factors seems to derive from cultural, theological or psychological perspectives on what is considered to be personal or social failure. The 'failure syndrome' often first appears in the process of determining whose 'fault' it is that the baby fails to appear. (A major step forward will have been taken when the word 'fault' ceases to apply in any discussion on childlessness.) The process of determining the cause of the inability to conceive is often a very fraught one, with the partners being required to undergo a range of examinations and tests to find out the source of the difficulty. This kind of examination may be a prerequisite to the attempt, too, to become an adoptive parent when, after the physical reasons have been established, the applicants go through further processes of selection and approval.

Parker[5] has suggested that all this activity implies an unconscious drive towards the search for an ideal state; we suggest that, also unconsciously, some childless couples may regard their inability to reproduce despite their great longing to do so as some kind of divine retribution for past or imagined transgressions, and the tests and obstacles become bearable as proof of good faith or of contrition, the successful completion of which may be linked with a surrogate absolution.

Carole Smith[6] refers to evidence from everyday popular and professional language to support her view that there exists widespread insensitivity to some of the basic issues. She cites the use of the words 'natural' being applied to the biological parents with the implied corollary that adoptive parenting is less real or natural. Lois Raynor[7] describes the insecurity felt by some adoptive parents who, despite the legal ties of adoption, believe they have less right to parent their children than biological parents would have.

Couple these factors with possible fantasies associated with the 'theft' of children from their biological parents, a notion supported by writers who like Alvin Shorr[8] have discussed the 'redistribution' of the population from poor biological parents to materially-secure adopters, and the weight of pressures upon would-be adopters becomes formidable; not only do they 'fail' in the human reproductive stakes, they may then be called upon to establish themselves as 'super-good' in their quest for acceptance as substitute parents. It is no wonder that many of them prefer to keep their intentions to themselves, especially now when the secondary 'failure' rate, that of actually having a child placed with them, is so high. For those who do manage it and succeed in adopting, it is not altogether surprising if many of them afterwards want nothing more than to put the whole business out of their minds. From the child's point of view, however, the subsequent reluctance to open the subject up for discussion can, as we have already suggested, be unhelpful.

Once again, the implications for helping professionals (and for concerned friends and relations, too) are serious. The state of childlessness can be glossed over as simplistically or uncritically as the state of illegitimacy, and with much the same kind of unconstructive results. We are not suggesting that the processes and events of adoptive parenthood have to be constantly at the forefront of people's minds any more than those of biological parenthood and birth. What we do suggest, however, is that a climate within which adoption and its ramifications are discussed without embarrassment or fear will more likely to lead to emotional security for all involved; the first requirement in reaching this stage is that a more honest acknowledgement of some of the problematic issues should form a part of a widespread programme of information and education. Social workers are particularly well placed to take the initiative in promoting such development.

Identity
Inextricably linked with 'telling' is the development in the adopted person of a sense of identity. Kornitzer[9] reached the heart of the matter with her suggestion that however open and honest adopters may be with a child, this sense of identity will be incomplete without detailed information about the birth parents.

Motivation in all our respondents was clearly related to issues of identity and 'belonging'. However, objectives were unclear, highly conflicting and complex and, as discussed earlier, this difference may reflect the timing of the research contact. There were, for example, contradictions in the objectives stated at the time of counselling and later at the time of the research interviews. In some cases further differences were observed between what respondents said and what they actually did.

For example, one woman stated that she had simply wanted to know where she was born but much later admitted that what she really wanted was information about her biological parents which would help to complete her perception of herself. All the respondents without exception initially claimed very tentative and modest objectives. It appeared that for many, underlying objectives and feelings could only be acknowledged in the context of sanctions or approval of others.

Records of respondents' histories and their activities in the search for information suggest that their actions were affected by a number of key factors; these were:

whether adoptive parents were alive or dead
attitude of spouse/close friends
real or assumed attitudes of adopters
attitude of social worker/counsellor
mobility; and practical obstructions to the search process
biographical information already available.

As some of these factors changed or modified, so did the objectives and actions of the respondents. One respondent voiced the feelings of the majority when she said that she felt 'everyone wants you to leave it alone', and described the sanctions applied by family and friends and, implicitly, even by social workers. Further confirmation of this was obtained in the follow-up group when respondents who had consistently stated the simple formal objectives of obtaining their original birth certificate or securing biographical information only, were able in the safety and support of the group to express a long-repressed desire to meet their birth parents.

All this is not to deny the potency of an unhappy adoption experience as a driving force in the search for origins. It is rather to emphasise that regardless of adoption experience the majority of adopted people will have an overwhelming need to know as much as possible about and probably to meet, if only once, their birth parent, purely for reasons of establishing their identity. This need for information and for meeting birth parents therefore seems to relate to the objective state of adoption. The concept of 'good' or 'bad' adoption experience in any case seems to be based on very insecure foundations, for as Goffman[10] has illustrated in his work on stigma, it *is* very convenient to be able to attribute misfortune and undesirable characteristics to a circumstance such as adoption. The majority of respondents had, because of the secrecy and evasiveness they experienced, developed the attitude that adoption was shameful and abnormal. Triseliotis' work confirmed this finding,[11] and some of his examples of ignorance and prejudice are quoted earlier. He further stated that this attitude was 'reinforced by community attitudes' and supported the finding, repeatedly confirmed in the course of this study, that adopted people are often reluctant to reveal their adoptive status even to close friends and family.

Two graphic examples of overcoming this reluctance occurred in the context of the follow-up group. The first was a young male respondent, an attractive extrovert personality, well able to relate and commun-icate, and with a very loving and satisfying family life. After two meetings the realisation dawned that he had never been able to tell his children aged six and nine, that he was adopted. He now felt that he should and could make this disclosure. The second example, a female respondent aged 40, also a warm outgoing personality, was even more dramatic. Through the process of searching and counselling she said she now felt able to talk to anyone of her adoption without embarrassment, or fear of their reaction. Her description of the feelings of pain and guilt, and then the sheer relief following revelation, can perhaps be compared with descriptions of homosexuals 'coming out'.

In his work on stigma Goffman[12] explores a variety of concepts relevant to the adoption situation. The problems for adopted people and their feelings about illegitimacy and difference from most other children are of course compounded by the fact that the other parties to adoption are themselves stigmatised: the birth parents were un-married, conceived a child outside marriage, or were unable to keep their child; the adoptive parents were unable to produce children of their own or chose not to and were consequently considered 'odd', or at least 'different'. Thus the three sets of people involved in adoption do not meet the normative expectations of society. As Goffman has stated:

> Failure or success at maintaining such norms has a very direct effect on the psychological integrity of the individual.

The many strategies employed by stigmatised individuals and described by Goffman had been, and still were, employed by the majority of our respondents and their families, in particular the control of information and protection within the domestic circle.

Of particular interest is the way in which school is often identified by Goffman with 'stigma learning', and the useful notion of a biography in the community. There were numerous examples in our study of respondents first finding out or first learning to cope with their stigma in school or in the immediate locality.

There were even examples of adopters attempting to move to areas where there would be no community biography so that a pretence of biological parenthood could be maintained.

Another pattern relevant to many adopted people is that of becoming aware of stigmatisation later in life. This involves individuals in a reorganisation of their 'view of the past'. Goffman says that such individuals (as, for example, those who first find out about their adoption as an adolescent or young adult) have already thoroughly learned about the normal and the stigmatised long before having to see themselves as deficient, and presumably will have a special problem in re-identifying themselves and 'a special likelihood of developing disapproval of self.'

Jane Rowe[13] explored some of these issues in 1970 when discussing the realities of adoptive parenthood. In asserting that little attention has been paid by writers or social workers to the philosophical, sociological and psychological bases of adoption, she grasps the nettle of largely unresolved questions fundamental to the feelings of shame and abnormality. For, as she concludes, 'unless social workers themselves reach a clear understanding of the realities of adoption and the adoption relationship, they will not be able to help the adopters to do so.'

Goffman suggests three solutions to the 'normative predicament':[14] acceptance of difference; alienation from the community; and a combination of strategies of control of information, secrecy and collusion in not claiming acceptance. While these solutions may enable the stigmatised individual to operate more or less effectively in social situations, they do not in any way help to eliminate the all-pervasive feelings of shame and embarrassment surrounding adoption. Several of our respondents even felt that adoption is an untenable concept, inevitably breeding pretence and dishonesty.

In the light of this evidence, the best way forward would seem to be along lines indicated by Rowe,[15] that is, a fundamental rethink of philosophical, sociological and psychological bases of adoption and a serious attempt to educate public attitudes and better equip social workers to engage with the issues and their practical implications.

'Secrets'

The theme of secrets ran powerfully through our research. For all respondents, the opportunity to spend time openly and specifically discussing adoption – particularly their adoption – was a new one. The secrecy with which adoption is associated probably develops from a number of different sources but illegitimacy seems to be a powerful one. It would be a mistake, in our view, to reject this on the grounds that our present-day liberated, sophisticated society is more tolerant and accepting than in the past. Such a social climate may well prevail at a general level of abstraction. When such matters concern oneself, however, it appears that people are influenced by deeper and more traditional attitudes, and social uncertainty results. As a further example of the power with which other, older social attitudes continue to influence contemporary thinking and behaviour, an *Observer* leader (8.2.87), responding to the inadequacy of a sentence for an offence of rape, noted that '. . . attitudes to women, even among the educated, are often primitive, insensitive and insulting'.

Social workers and others might have been lulled into a misguided sense of complacency founded upon an inaccurate expectation of public enlightenment and tolerance towards illegitimacy. The view that little or no shame attaches either to the unmarried mother (for it is usually she and not the father who seeks help) or her baby might be an optimistic one. But instead of opening up this area for discussion and facing its implications, the social worker moves on to discuss the 'real' problems of sustenance and survival. And indeed, these often are very real problems, for social policy and welfare provisions are in many respects discriminatory and unsupportive. Attention to them, however, should not preclude appraisal of either the social context within which they operate or the personal, emotional and psychological reactions they produce. It is relatively recently (May 1983) that Jane Streather, drawing on her considerable experience of work with the National Council for One Parent Families, said in the course of a BBC radio broadcast that not only were illegitimate children disadvantaged in contemporary British society; they may be regarded as 'different, inferior and doomed'. Moreover, the term 'bastard' is still used pejoratively. Our respondents suggested, only half-jokingly, that if anything were to be written about their experiences it should be called 'Bastards Anonymous'.

There were many indications of the potency of their illegitimate status for our respondents. Male respondents quoted examples of wildly extreme responses, in their youth, to being called 'bastard'. Less typically, one had learned to defend himself in more subtle ways by quoting from a John Wayne film: 'Mine was an accident of birth; you made it all by yourself.' Allusions to 'bad blood' and doubtful 'character' had also been experienced:

> I think they expected that you, if your mother had loose morals, might turn out to be the same.

It might have been easier for the women to express their feelings and experiences – they were, after all, successful wives and mothers now, demonstrably able to give the lie to the prejudices and fantasies to which they might have been subject. It might have been more difficult for men to live down the unconscious guilt by association: aware of, and sensitive to, ideas which prevail about unmarried mothers (their unmarried mothers), it is not possible for them to demonstrate the lack of substance in such views in the way that women can. Nevertheless, they may retain within themselves distorted images about their 'birth mothers' whilst, at the same time, still experiencing a deep emotional need to know more about them. (The men in the study especially expressed interest in finding out about their mothers.) The tension this conflict might produce could result in a high degree of denial or ambivalence, possibly contributing to the fact that fewer men than women have taken steps to gain access to their birth records. This is, of course, speculative and as such is offered tentatively.

The sexually discriminatory nature of explicit or implicit attitudes towards unmarried parenthood are well known. It is not intended to pursue the politics of feminism as applied to illegitimacy but it cannot be ignored as a perspective on the influences on the adopted child as he or she grows up. Our respondents had certainly received more negative messages about their mothers than their fathers and it seems likely that despite increasing sexual equality, it is still the unmarried mother who is in danger of becoming the target for opprobrium in a way that the unmarried father is not.

Women members of the group were, not surprisingly perhaps, particularly sensitive to this. One woman obtained general endorsement for the view that: 'She's a slag, but he's a hero.'

If this is the received perception, it would not be surprising if one's sense of self, derived from one's birth identity, were to be influenced by it. Several women in the group agreed that as teenagers they had been acutely aware of parental fears that they would 'get into trouble': 'It's as though they expect us to produce lots of illegitimate children.'

We do not wish to present a view of the unmarried father as necessarily carefree, irresponsible and emotionally unscathed, though some men do conform to such a model. Previous experience in work with numbers of young men about to become unmarried fathers, however, does not permit such crude and simplistic assertion. We merely highlight the implications of sexist attitudes towards illegitimacy and our evidence suggests that for those involved in our study, a fairly high level of anxiety existed which was based upon a fear that their mothers had been promiscuous:

Having an illegitimate child does not imply loose morals.

It does to society.

Everybody thinks your mother must have been on the game.

It could be argued that this fragment of conversation represents a skewed interpretation of social attitudes; 'society' does not, in reality, make such judgements and the views expressed may be, quite simply, mistaken. It is then necessary to ask where such distorted perceptions have come from. If one has been at the receiving end of negative or mixed social messages for long periods of time it is understandable if sensitivity and suspicion become heightened – comparison with experiences of members of minority ethnic groups, for example, can illustrate the ways in which this happens. Moreover, social work practice recognises and understands that perceptions, even when faulty, may be no less real to the individual holding them: 'feelings are facts' and are not to be dispensed with merely on the basis of intellectual discussion.

Although powerful emotions relating to birth mothers were identified and the majority of respondents expressed the wish to know more about their mothers, it would not be true to suggest that all concern and attention was mother-focused. For at least one (female) member of the group it was very important:

> . . . to know who my father was. I was very relieved to be told that he had been a perfectly normal young man from a good and respectable family.

The fact that many adopted people seem preoccupied with mothers is perhaps linked with the cultural emphasis placed upon mother-child relationships in our society, with the significance of the father's role and importance to the child sometimes wrongly and unhelpfully played down. Haimes and Timms[16] also found in their study that most respondents wanted to find out more about their mothers but suggested that a lesser expectation of discovering much about their fathers could lead them to concentrate their efforts upon their mothers:

> I know I'm going to come up against a brick wall as far as my father is concerned and that really is as important to me as my mother.

Two female members of our group established contact with their fathers. In one situation the contact was sustained but was somewhat unsatisfying in that the adopted person remained more eager to trace her mother. Although the father was very warm and welcoming of his daughter, she felt ambivalent about the contact. In the second situation, the initial contact with one parent led to a reunion with the other; both had married other partners but it seemed clear that a great deal of unresolved emotional material existed between them, some of which they were able to sort out with their daughter as an important and involved participant in the process.

Very closely linked with the question of illegitimate status was the generally-shared apprehension concerning the actual circumstances of the group members' conceptions. Most people speculate at some time or another about their parents' sexual relationship and those brought up by their mother and father assume that their conception occurred as a result of love within a stable and optimistic situation. Even if subsequently their parents separate, most people believe that they were glad to have their children and that they were welcomed into the world and their births celebrated as happy and joyous events. For some adopted people, however, it may be very difficult to base their existence and identity on such firm ground and it emerged in the course of the group discussions that a good deal of fear existed concerning their parents' sexual encounters: 'You don't like to talk about it but you do wonder about your parents' relationship.'

Almost all our respondents imagined themselves to be the outcome of casual sex – 'promiscuous' and 'one night stands' were the terms often used. It is difficult for those who have not had to do it to comprehend basing one's existence on such concepts; but it is not difficult to see how the Goffman-esque concept of the 'spoiled identity'[17] might emerge.

Counselling
The counselling process is of particular interest not least because of the implications of the full implementation of the Children Act 1975.* It is useful to recall here that the counselling arrangements in the department in which our study was conducted were likely to compare very favourably with arrangements in any social services department.

---

*Section 1 of the Children Act 1975, implemented in 1988, placed a duty upon local authorities to provide counselling for people with problems relating to adoption.

The social workers were experienced specialists in fostering and adoption and had received special preparation for the task. Respondents were, on the whole, quite generously disposed towards the social workers and generally favoured the concept of counselling; however, there were clearly very serious limitations as to the helpfulness of the process.

Several factors appeared to contribute to this failure and some stemmed from existing feelings, previously discussed, about respondents' adoptive status. Compounding these were their image of a social services department: most respondents had preconceived perceptions of the role of social services and feelings that departments existed for those with pressing practical needs and serious family crises. Their feelings that social services departments had more important work to do and were not really geared to dealing with problems of a less obvious nature were confirmed by the implicit 'messages' they perceived coming from the department, for example that social workers were often difficult to contact and could not see them immediately, and that interviews took place in rather dilapidated offices. Several felt that an interview in their own home would have been more appropriate. Further difficulties arose from the social workers' generally non-directive, reflective approach which unintentionally reinforced adopted people's expectations of disapproval and led to distortions in perceptions of the social workers' attitudes.

It was clear that most members of the group needed and expected much more practical advice and help than was generally forthcoming. This deficiency made them vulnerable to professional tracing services, and there was evidence that some respondents had considered seeking help from commercial enterprises of a possibly dubious nature.

As Day[18] found in 1979, counselling served a useful purpose in increasing awareness of relevant issues, and in giving support and approval to the 'good intentions and responsible attitudes' of the majority. It also served a useful purpose in reducing the possibilities of precipitate action on the part of a small minority.

Linked with the general reluctance which people feel at having to consult social workers is the public view of social work and its practitioners, especially as presented in some sections of the media. This might be even more of an issue now than in the late 1970s and early 1980s: in the intervening period there has been a hardening of social attitudes which has not been conducive to furthering the social work cause and there have, of course, been a number of well-publicised child abuse tragedies. So social work is generally identified with human casualty and with the lower end of the class scale. It possesses, therefore, quite a high element of stigma and for the respondents there had already been too much of that. This is not to be construed as an argument for not involving social workers in this area of practice. It does, however, underline the importance of the profession seeking to improve its public image, not out of any sense of aggrandisement but because a failure to provide a confident rebuttal to some of the more damaging public portrayals may actually harm users of the service. It is an absurd situation when clients, already stigmatised in these times of sturdy independence by the need to seek some form of assistance, perceive themselves as further penalised as a result of this contact. No one assumes that people only visit their solicitor when they are about to be charged with an offence. It would be a big step forward if social work clients could come to view their dealings with social workers with equanimity and not as something of which to be ashamed.

A further difficulty for our respondents was the fact that social workers had such heavy caseloads. Agency priorities were defined in terms of risk, and this was sometimes made quite explicit:

> My counsellor was an excellent person but she told me quite bluntly that she was very busy and had other jobs to do, and small children were obviously more important than my problem. I cannot criticise her, she was excellent, but I felt I was being a nuisance, selfish . . .

More typically, respondents were aware of the pressures of other work which were placed upon the social workers:

> . . . perhaps I would ring her up and need to talk because I'd just found something out, and she would be in court . . . You get the feeling you can be a nuisance if you push it anymore.

This kind of experience, which was common, caused the respondents to regard their entitlement to social work time and attention as much less legitimate than that of people 'with real problems'. This served to confirm for many of them the feeling that they should just be grateful for what they already had in life, and that to want to know about their origins was, as one of them put it, 'a real ego trip' (an unconscious irony) and a piece of self-indulgence. It was in the context of a

94

particularly distressed discussion of this topic at one of the group meetings that it became necessary for we researchers briefly to step outside our negotiated role. In the interests of the individuals it seemed essential to endorse the validity of their need to answer the question 'who am I?' and their entitlement to professional time and concern in this quest.

This was particularly relevant as all except one of the people in our group had major problems in discussing their origins with their adoptive parents. Their husbands and wives and immediate families often felt threatened or excluded, or simply could not understand their need to know. They consistently felt that the unspoken messages they received were to 'leave well alone' and became reluctant to talk to anyone.

Sadly, this problem seemed to be compounded by social workers who did not sufficiently recognise the need to sanction what had come to be viewed as self-indulgence. Practical problems for adopted people were exacerbated by bad feelings about, for example, using family money to pursue their search for origins. Train fares, letters, and telephone calls can become prohibitive for families on fairly tight budgets, and expenditure on such activities can add to the guilt and conflict associated with the search. Social work departments ought to be able to match that personal investment with something similar in terms of professional support and attention.

In our view the respondents did not have unrealistic expectations and were acutely sensitive to other demands on social workers. Within those parameters, however, they needed and could have received more active encouragement and acknowledgement of their claims on professional time. There is obviously therefore a need for agencies to recognise this fact in planning and seeking resources. For many respondents the counselling process was the first and only opportunity to talk with an informed, interested and objective person about their adoption experience.

In this context the rationale for 'compulsory' or 'optional' counselling in access to birth records warrants further consideration. According to existing law, this relates simply to the timing of the adoption, that is before or after November 1976 when the law changed, and the problems which might arise as a result of retroactive legislation. However, the value of a counselling service derives from factors associated with feelings about adoption and identity, and factual knowledge and information about legislation, organisations and processes. While it is acknowledged that adopters and others associated with adoption should be more aware of the adopted person's rights to certain information post-1975, it seems unlikely that there would be significant differences in the need for counselling.

Health of adopters

Some histories included distressing separations and even serious trauma at a very early age because of periods of hospitalisation or difficulties in the marriage which, with hindsight, it is felt could have been avoided with more care and greater objectivity at the time of approval and placement. Problems arising from negative attitudes of extended families, or from gross physical differences between adopters and adopted people, were equally foreseeable and preventable. This latter point should help to inform practice in transracial adoptions.

Summary of practical implications of findings

Many implications for practice have already emerged from this study. In summary the major issues of particular relevance for social work practice are as follows:

Selection of adopters

The ability of adoptive parents to deal openly and honestly with the adopted child in all matters, particularly those relating to his or her origins, was seen by all respondents as the single most important attribute.

Assessment of this quality in potential applicants is not only extremely difficult but, if the findings of this study can be generally applied, is also a task in which we have singularly failed.

Some of the most obvious yardsticks would be the applicants' performance in communicating about sensitive issues with each other and with the social worker. If there is any doubt, based upon this and upon other measures which may be devised, then the findings of this study would firmly suggest rejection of the applicants.

The indications from our study are that those adopters thought at the time of placement to have the appropriate potential for this task frequently did not, and skilled help is obviously required if adopted people are not to suffer serious problems in the development of identity.

The solution to the problem of the provision of a skilled and acceptable (to adopters) counselling service is beyond the scope of this small study. Some of the issues are discussed briefly below. It must be hoped that with the full implementation of comprehensive counselling services in all aspects of adoption consideration would be given to these issues, but there is little evidence to suggest that this is the case. Provision of the appropriate degree and range of skills will of course require detailed consideration, but the crucial and much more problematic issue is likely to be how to deliver the service appropriately and acceptably.

Associated with issues of selection and counselling are questions of training and monitoring. Should there be an obligatory training period before a child is placed with adopters, and should there be an obligatory monitoring process designed to ensure the rights to information of the adopted child? On the first question there would appear to be much in favour. Adoptive parents do not have the preparation of pregnancy, although most have a similar or longer waiting period between approval and placement. However helpful this period might be as a mental preparation for having a child, it is unlikely that without experienced help potential adopters can adequately prepare for the profound differences between adoptive and biological parenthood. We therefore suggest that this difference should be explicitly recognised from the beginning and that adopters should not be considered unless they are prepared to engage in the training/ preparatory process. This could even constitute a second phase in their approval as adopters.

Training/preparation is not of course envisaged as an exercise which would eliminate those of an average or low academic ability, but would rather be designed to identify and develop qualities of open communication, and rigorously to work through feelings about infertility, illegitimacy and adoption. We would also suggest that adult adopted people could be recruited to assist in the training/preparation process.

While the negative experiences of some of our group prompt suggestions of monitoring, this is not felt to be practically or legally viable. Much more desirable would be a system as suggested above which would positively strengthen selection, preparation and counselling.

Compilation and management of biographical information for adopted people

The findings of this study lead to a number of recommendations:

a) guidelines or regulations should be issued by central government on the information to be collated and recorded at the time of placement, and on the keeping and disclosure of agency and court records to establish and ensure consistency;

b) a dossier of detailed information should be compiled and given to the adopters, and a copy retained by the agency. The information to be recorded should include personal histories and physical descriptions of birth parents; information about their extended families; medical information about birth families; the nature of the relationship between the birth parents; detailed information about the birth and early life of the child; as many photographs as possible of the birth parents and extended families and the child prior to the adoption;

c) agencies should be able and prepared to provide information and counselling to adopted people of any age who may seek their assistance.

Advice and help for adopted people

Is the concept of 'one door on which to knock' viable? Can social services departments provide high quality work in specialist areas? Can the image and service delivery model of social services departments accommodate clients requiring an essentially therapeutic service albeit with some practical overtones?

While social services departments clearly have the potential to provide the counselling service required by adopted people, and indeed others involved in adoption, their desire or ability to modify their image and approach to provide an adequate and acceptable service for those with predominantly therapeutic needs must be questioned. However, as the expertise is present in local authorities, in our view they are best placed to do this work. A rethink of organisation and presentation of the services would nonetheless seem to be indicated.

Whatever pattern of service delivery to this group is eventually decided, it is strongly recommended that group counselling and self-help are fundamental parts of the methodology adopted. A nationally co-ordinated information and linking service for adopted people and birth parents who wish to register their willingness to be contacted, as recommended by NORCAP, is wholeheartedly endorsed.

In the preparation of workers to provide the service, close attention should be paid to developing their detailed practical knowledge of record systems of agencies, courts and the General Register Office, as well as familiarity with the structure of electoral registers and any other sources of accessible information held by organisations such as the DOH and DSS, the armed services and churches, etc.

Cultural implications, and the education and training of social workers and others
Is is possible to influence public attitudes and understanding to the extent that secrecy and shame in this area will be eliminated?

The problems of public attitudes and the education and training of professionals appear to be inextricably linked and are probably rooted in the lack of a sound philosophical, sociological and emotional basis for the concept of substitute parenting. Perhaps this derives in turn from a too narrow view in our culture of 'normal' parenting. Until these questions are resolved it will be difficult to further develop the practice skills of social workers in the reinforcement of the validity and value of substitute parenting and the development of a sense of identity in this context. Some improvements in the practice of other professionals such as teachers, doctors and health visitors could be made relatively easily by the introduction to their basic training of material designed to improve knowledge and understanding. At a fairly simple level it would be widely beneficial if more acceptable language could be introduced for describing family relationships which do not conform to the norm. Terminology currently in use is variable, awkward and often unintentionally denigrating.

As may have been expected, a study such as ours tends to raise more questions than it answers. Its greatest aspiration can only be to add in a small way to a developing pool of knowledge about the feelings and experiences of adopted people. It has provided further confirmation that an adopted person's quest for origins does not usually derive from revenge or negative feelings, but from a powerful drive to create a sense of identity from two sets of parents and two families, sometimes even from two distinct cultural backgrounds. It also confirms the continuing need for research in these areas, and particularly into one of Cooper's questions: 'If it is established that family placement is appropriate as the preferred form of treatment, then is adoption so much more emotionally secure than fostering that a move towards adoption is justified?'[19]

Discussion with respondents has been for we researchers a revelation and a privilege. The constraints of space and indeed our own limitations have determined that so much of what was so openly shared by respondents cannot be fully reproduced or adequately interpreted here. However, if respondents wished to convey one dominant message it would be their inalienable right to knowledge of who they are and where they have come from. The task of legislators, social administrators and social workers must be to uphold and develop that right, and to seek to inform public knowledge and understanding to full acceptance of the validity of the adoptive family.

References

1 Chennells P *Explaining adoption to your adopted child* BAAF, 1988.

2 Houghton D and Houghton P *Coping with childlessness* Allen and Unwin, 1984.

3 *Independent* 10 January 1987.

4 Goffman E *Stigma: notes on the management of spoiled identity* Penguin Books, 1963.

5 Parker R A (ed) *Caring for separated children* Macmillan, 1980.

6 Smith C *Adoption and fostering: why and how* BASW/Macmillan, 1984.

7 Raynor L *The adopted child comes of age* Allen and Unwin, 1980.

8 Shorr A *Children and decent people* Allen and Unwin, 1975.

9 Kornitzer M 'The adopted adolescent and the sense of identity' *Child adoption* 65, 1971.

10 See 4 above.

11 Triseliotis J *In search of origins* Routledge & Kegan Paul, 1973.

12 See 4 above.

13 Rowe J 'The realities of adoptive parenthood' *Child adoption* 59, 1970.

14 See 4 above.

15 See 13 above.

16 Haimes E and Timms N *Adoption, identity and social policy* Gower, 1985.

17 See 4 above.

18 Day C 'General register office study' in Hall T (ed) *Access to birth records* ABAFA, 1980.

19 Cooper JD *Patterns of family placement: current issues in adoption and fostering* National Children's Bureau, 1978.

5 Human fertilisation and embryology

After the publication of the Report of the Committee of Inquiry[1] which she chaired, Mary Warnock wrote a new introductory chapter to a book which reproduced the Report.[2] In this she quoted from the philosopher Hume, who wrote that morality was 'more properly felt than judged of' – the notion being that the distinctions between right and wrong are drawn less by reason than by moral sense, that is by what feels right. This wise comment seems to epitomise the dilemmas faced by the Warnock Committee, and now to be faced by Parliament. It is already patently clear from the report and the white paper *Human fertilisation and embryology: a framework for legislation*[3] that no absolute moral or legal precepts exist which can guide the intense arguments which will surely rage when the bill which derives from the white paper eventually emerges into the parliamentary spotlight. In another context, that of brain transplant, with which embryo and semen donation might be seen to share some common issues, Dr Jonathan Miller has been quoted as saying that 'moral judgements are not absolute, they are negotiable'.[4]

What is clear, however, is that scientific experiment and medical practice in this country in donor insemination (DI, previously known as AID or artificial insemination by donor), in-vitro fertilisation (IVF) and embryo research have existed and continue, largely unregulated, on a significant scale. Third-party surrogacy arrangements also appear to have continued, despite the fact that commercial surrogacy arrangements were outlawed by the Surrogacy Arrangements Act 1985. For example, in July 1988 the Department of Health announced an inquiry into claims by an organisation called Triangle that large numbers of surrogate babies were being born and that more were planned.[5] Moreover, this practice was held by the alleged perpetrators to be within the law as no fees were being charged.

The only regulation at the present time is provided by a Voluntary Licensing Authority (VLA) which regards its work as temporary and itself favours the establishment of a statutory authority. The VLA was established jointly by the Royal College of Obstetricians and Gynaecologists and the Medical Research Council in 1985 and invites centres engaged in relevant medical practice or scientific research to apply for approval and licence.

Events surrounding Warnock and the white paper
In 1982 the government set up a Committee of Inquiry chaired by Mrs Mary (now Baroness) Warnock, Mistress of Girton College, Cambridge, and an eminent moral philosopher. Its terms of reference were 'to consider recent and potential developments in medicine and science related to human fertilisation and embryology; to consider what policies and safeguards should be applied, including consideration of the social, ethical and legal implications of these developments; and to make recommendations.'

The committee reported in 1984 and we will return to the recommendations and subsequent events in due course. However, it is worth considering events preceding the report, as the practices it sought to examine were already well established, some indeed having quite a lengthy history.

Warnock and the authors of the white paper accept that surrogacy is a long-standing phenomenon, probably going back generations. Both condemn the practice but admit the difficulty in controlling it. The Baby Cotton case* was the first to arouse major public attention and conern in this country, and it led directly to the Surrogacy Arrangements Act 1985. This makes it illegal for a third party to take part in negotiations for a commercial surrogacy arrangement or to offer to do so. It also prohibits advertising of or for surrogacy services. As we have already seen, however, it is claimed that surrogacy arrangements continue on a similar or even greater scale than hitherto.

It is also clear that the practice of donor insemination has existed for some considerable time. For example, in 1983 Snowden et al[6]

---

*On 4 January 1985 Mrs Kim Cotton gave birth to the first British baby known to be born as a result of a commercial arrangement with a surrogate parenting agency. She had been artificially inseminated with the sperm of a man who, with his wife, was to pay her an agreed fee of £6,500. The baby was made subject to a Place of Safety Order and later became a Ward of Court. Subsequently the father (who had no rights because the baby was illegitimate) and his wife adopted the baby. See Cotton K and Winn D *Baby Cotton: for love and money* Dorling Kindersley, 1985.

examined the experience of 899 couples who underwent DI between 1940 and 1980. One objective of the research was to study the experience of individual families. Unfortunately, as a result of the intense secrecy surrounding DI, this was restricted to families whose children had left home or were too young to understand the significance of the researchers' visit. The researchers gained information about seven adults who had been told in their late teens and twenties that they had been conceived as a result of DI. Here they record similar findings to adoption research.

Of the 57 couples who had given birth to a child five or fewer years ago, 48 had resolved not to tell their child, three had decided to tell and six were undecided. Some had told friends and relatives and generally received understanding and sympathy. Many had agonised over such confidences and the implications both of children finding out inadvertently and of themselves being caught up in a never-ending web of deceit. These stresses, and those arising from the 'stigma' of childlessness and infertility are explored in the research, and reflect the same feelings recorded in adoption research about couples who have sought to resolve their childlessness in that way. The researchers' comments make it easy to understand the extreme pressures upon medical practitioners to want to respond and help their patients: ' . . . the frustration of their desire to have children is extremely hurtful and a feeling of sadness permeates their whole lives'.

In recent years these feelings have increasingly come to be expressed in terms of the rights of individuals to have children. In 1984, for example, two books in particular presented this view: *Coping with childlessness* by Diane and Peter Houghton,[7] and *The gift of a child* by Robert and Elizabeth Snowden.[8] The latter even went so far as to assert that ' . . . the right to a child is enshrined in the United Nations Charter of Human Rights'. This theme also emerged in the Warnock Report which recorded evidence drawing upon Articles 8 and 12 of the European Convention on Human Rights which guarantee a respect for family life and the right to found a family. The Report states: 'it has been argued that these provisions create a right to take full advantage of the techniques which are available to alleviate infertility'.

The National Association for the Childless (NAC) was established in 1976 and has been an important exponent of these views. NAC campaigns for 'improved fertility services and better public understanding of the need to help people have their own children'. It gives individual advice about fertility problems and personal feelings and concerns about treatment and coping with childlessness. Members can also benefit from group support and from a comprehensive inform-ation service about all aspects of infertility and treatment.[9]

Whether or not views about rights to have children find favour, the development of organisations and the emergence of articulate individuals is crucial to proper debate to ensure consideration of all the important issues. The list of organisations submitting evidence to the Warnock Committee provides ample proof of the vigorous represen-tation of every religious and professional perspective together with the interests of childless adults and those concerned about research into the prevention of disability. Only agencies broadly representing social work ethics and experience have drawn attention to the rights of the 'child': indeed, what has been conspicuously absent is an informed body equally dedicated to ensuring proper identification and consider-ation of the rights and needs of people conceived by artificial means. Modern science has made it possible for such people to have four or five 'parents', some of whom might have been dead before conception. In some circumstances an individual could have two genetic donating parents, a surrogate mother and two nurturing parents. Given the breakdown of the partnership of the nurturing parents, a possibility not difficult to contemplate in terms of present social trends, the child could pass to new nurturing parents – a combination of genetic and nurturing parentage which could be confusing and troubling to the most stable of individuals. Unlimited numbers of genetic siblings would of course also be a possibility.

The event which has perhaps most captured public attention and raised awareness of the need for very serious consideration of ethical and moral issues was the first 'test tube baby' in July 1978. Writing in the *Spectator* in January 1988, Michael Trend said: 'Drs Robert Edwards and Patrick Steptoe, who *produced* the baby [our emphasis], recently celebrated their thousandth such birth . . . That first birth, however, ushered in a debate on the ethics of modern medicine that was greatly intensified as the first ripples spread widely from homely Oldham to all parts of the world . . . Suddenly all sorts of things became possible.' These possibilities included the development of embryos purely for research purposes and the screening of embryos for genetic defects, both of which are now fact.

The apparent world-wide decline in fertility is also worthy of note:

for example, a study conducted in the Bristol area concluded that 17 per cent of couples were unsuccessful after two years of trying to conceive.[10] We know that in the UK there are some 27,500 women who have been unsuccessful in becoming pregnant, and that there is evidence on a world-wide basis that sperm counts are decreasing due to environmental toxins. The relevance of increasing infertility to our present considerations is of course the likelihood of even greater pressure being brought to bear upon scientific research and medical practice to facilitate the creation of families. Perhaps equally predictable may be the further submergence of the voice of the person created via medical expertise in response to infertility?

Controversy has raged about embryo research since 1978. Enoch Powell's Unborn Children (Protection) Bill received a successful second reading in February 1985 but eventually fell because of lack of parliamentary time. Kenneth Hind's Private Member's Bill with the purpose of protecting human embryos from research received a similar fate in 1988.

In March 1988 'pro-life' MPs launched a campaign to ban all research on human embryos with a report from the group's medical and scientific advisory committee. Erwin Chargaff, the distinguished biochemist and pioneer of DNA research, now retired from the University of Columbia, is one of a number of eminent scientists who have argued against such research in very strong terms. He said in a contribution to the report: 'What I see coming is a gigantic slaughterhouse, a molecular Auschwitz, in which valuable enzymes, hormones and so on will be extracted instead of gold teeth.'[11]

In November of the same year a new campaign organisation was launched, called 'Progress'. This aims to provide information and correct misinformation concerning 'pre-embryo' (that is the first 14 days after fertilisation) research. The campaign has the support of some 50 organisations representing the interests of the infertile, the disabled and those involved in family planning. Writing in the Spring 1989 edition of *Issues*, the magazine of NAC, Dr Virginia Bolton, chairperson of Progress, asserted that the 'campaign must win' and claimed that the debates on the white paper in the House of Lords on 15 January 1988 and the House of Commons on 4 February 1988 demonstrated a major shift of opinion to the support of pre-embryo research. The following arguments are put forward by Dr Bolton to support the necessity for pre-embryo research:

This research will help to provide a better understanding of human fertility, or infertility, and thus ultimately to improve the efficiency of assisted conception techniques. Thus, while many different figures are quoted as 'pregnancy rates' following attempts at assisted conception, the only figure that has any real meaning is the 'take home baby rate'. Despite the fact that it is now more than ten years since the birth of the world's first baby conceived by in-vitro fertilisation (IVF), the take home baby rate is still only nine per cent per treatment, in the best centres. When a couple embarks on IVF treatment, they are taking a gamble with the odds stacked against them. Research must be allowed to continue if this situation is to improve.

Research will also facilitate the development of techniques for the diagnosing of genetic diseases in the pre-embryo. For couples at high risk of transmitting a genetic disorder to their children, diagnosing such a disease before pregnancy would mean alleviation of the anguish caused by multiple terminations of affected pregnancies, or even resignation to a lifetime of childlessness. The successful development and perfection of such techniques, and their ultimate incorporation into clinical practice, depends on the use of human embryos in research.

In the absence of legislation such research is continuing anyway, and in December 1988 Dr Robert Winston, professor of fertility studies at the Hammersmith Hospital in London, announced a programme to carry out genetic screening of embryos to detect disabling conditions. This could not have been attempted if the bills referred to above had been successful, and the questions prompted by these advances are endless and add to the urgency for formal regulation to be fully considered and introduced. Decisions about whether or not to allow pre-embryo research are complex enough, but even more complex questions will be posed. For example, when genetic screening identifies that an embryo carries a predisposition for some disease or condition, what will determine life or death for that embryo? Some conditions will perhaps produce universal agreement about termination: it seems safe to assume, however, that others will not.

The recommendations of the Committee of Inquiry and the white paper

The main findings of the Report of the Committee of Inquiry, endorsed by the white paper, were that certain infertility treatments and research involving human embryos should be permitted *subject to statutory control by an independent body.* The treatments and practices under consideration were:

artificial insemination, or the placing of sperm inside a woman's vagina or womb by means other than sexual intercourse. AIH refers to the process using the husband or partner's sperm and DI using sperm from a donor. Approximately 1,700 children per year are born in the UK as a result of DI;

in-vitro fertilisation is a technique used where a woman has no fallopian tubes or where the tubes are blocked. A ripe egg, taken from the ovary before it is released naturally, is mixed with sperm in a dish (*in vitro*) so that fertilisation can occur. When the fertilised egg starts to develop it is placed in the womb. Because of the difficulty of the technique, more than one embryo is created and transferred. This is facilitated by the use of superovulatory drugs and has frequently resulted in multiple births. Extensions of the IVF technique are egg donation, which means that an infertile woman may be implanted with the egg of another woman which has been fertilised by her husband's sperm, and embryo donation which means that both egg and sperm have been donated. It is estimated that since 1978 over 1,200 births in the UK have involved IVF;

surrogacy involves one woman carrying a child for another with the intention that the child is handed over at birth. This can take a number of forms which may include the egg of the carrying mother being artificially fertilised by the commissioning father or a donor, the embryo being entirely a product of donation or entirely a product of the commissioning parents where the commissioning mother is unable to carry the pregnancy. In the latter case surrogacy would also of course be technically possible where a commissioning mother were able but unwilling to carry the pregnancy. No estimates are available of the numbers of surrogate births although claims have been made as mentioned above.

Since the Warnock Report was published there have inevitably been new developments. The white paper commented: ' . . . there have been several scientific and clinical developments in the UK and elsewhere.

None of them significantly affects the factual basis of the Warnock Report. They include improving techniques for preserving human embryos by freezing and developing methods of freezing eggs.'

The report made recommendations about surrogacy, the storage and disposal of human embryos and gametes (ie eggs and/or sperm), the status of children born following gamete or embryo donation, and the development of infertility services generally, including counselling. Each of these was included in the white paper and subsequently the bill with little modification. Consultation produced much agreement about some issues, particularly surrogacy; hence the 1985 Act.* The initial BAAF response to surrogacy, which was 'cautious but open minded', disapproving of commercial arrangements but accepting of non-commercial arrangements, was fairly typical at the time of Warnock. Careful consideration of the interests of the child, however, led to a more developed approach expressed in BAAF's July 1987 policy statement, summed up in the sentence: 'we cannot believe that it is right to create children with the deliberate intention of separating them from their birth mothers'.

Embryo research resulted in much disagreement and a further consultation document was issued in December 1986.[12] The consultation period ended in June 1987 and the white paper was published in November 1987. Some of the debate since that time has already been described in this chapter, and it is assumed that the intention expressed in the white paper that a free vote should be allowed on this issue is still the case.

It is now over two years since the publication of the white paper and five years since Warnock. The bill is now published (November 1989) but much is yet unknown about the government's intentions and will only emerge with detailed regulations. A number of observers have criticised the government for inaction. Michael Trend in the *Spectator* in January 1988 said: 'What the government has in effect done is to hand the problem over to the "experts" for five years in the hope that "they" will come up with some sort of authoritative position that will command popular support.' Similar sentiments were expressed by Melanie Phillips in the *Guardian*[13] when she said: 'And the failure to legislate on embryology undoubtedly solves other anxieties. For within

---

*This makes it an offence for a third party to take part in a commercial arrangement, or to offer to do so.

the Department of Health and the scientific establishment, where there are widespread sympathies for embryo research, there are fears that if the issue is let loose in Parliament, MPs might vote the wrong way and stop all embryo research. In the absence of a bill and a debate, meanwhile research is proceeding apace, sanctioned by the Voluntary Licensing Authority. It is the medical version of the created fact.'

As Lady Warnock herself commented later: 'All the other issues we had to consider seemed relatively trivial compared with this one, concerned as it is with a matter which nobody could deny is of central moral significance, the value of human life.'[14] This quite proper preoccupation with such an overwhelming issue is perhaps one explanation for the failure adequately to consider the offspring of human fertilisation and embryology after the embryonic stage. It might also explain why DI received such scant attention from the committee.

In an article published in 1986, McWhinnie expressed surprise that the committee seemed to have assumed that because DI 'was practised it was acceptable'.[15] She draws attention to the fact that 'what . . . is actually involved has never really been aired' and speculates that this may be because men, who have predominated in the post-Warnock debate, 'are uncomfortable about actually talking about it openly, either because of the donor aspect and/or the male infertility aspect'. She argues, rightly in our view, that there is an analogy with adoption, 'since the children in both cases are reared by parents other than both their genetic parents and because there is an artificially created situation where the adults in a child's world have information about the child that they can decide to share or withhold'. By implication this must also be true of egg donation. Further, she agrees with Mitchell[16] that the secrecy and deceit which are advocated as part of the DI procedures undermine the whole basis of our society in which family and kinship roles are based upon honesty and trust. Finally, she argues that children whose parentage derives wholly or partly from other than their nurturing parents 'have a right and need to be told this in a caring and thoughtful way, ideally by their parents.' She recognises the reality, however, that the implied admission of infertility will deter many parents from this course and thus advocates the introduction of legal rights similar to those existing for adopted people. The important point is also made that while the Warnock recommendations open the door for the first time to DI children they will not satisfy the

government will 'keep the situation under review' as 'attitudes to the anonymity of donors, however, may well change over time *as happened with adoption*' [our emphasis].
own genetic make up.'

The report recommendations, the white paper and the general debate in the media are all remarkable for their lack of detailed consideration of the rights, feelings and potential problems of the person created through sophisticated medical practices and often with a highly complex genetic heritage. That may not be surprising given the powerful interplay of strong personal feelings, energetic lobbies, vested interests and real and perplexing issues operating in this very difficult field, some of which we have attempted to describe. The implicit and consistent denial of what many would argue is an important issue cannot, however, be acceptable. It should be remembered, too, that this is not only an issue for the future: arguably it may already be an issue for some at least of the thousands of people in existence today as a result of sperm or embryo donation.

Warnock did little more than clarify the albeit important questions of legal status and legitimacy. The other critical questions of identity, psychological wholeness and rights to personal biographical information were completely fudged, as indeed they were in the white paper. The important question of whether there is a responsibility to the unborn child to determine fitness for parenthood before giving access to fertility procedures also received scant consideration in Warnock, and a cursory dismissal in the white paper. It is our contention that these issues warrant considerably more serious attention: we will seek here to indicate why.

Development of identity and the importance of biographical information

Reference was made in our Introduction to the fact that the government, like Warnock, recognises that there is an issue of access to biographical information for the 'child'. In our view, however, it is advanced with only limited appreciation of why this might be important. The white paper stance on the subject could fairly be said to be planted firmly on the fence with one ear to the ground. Inevitably such a stance means relative inaction, although the proposed introduction of rights of access to non-identifying information about donors is to be welcomed. There is also the proposition that the

111

requirements of rights, needs or legitimate curiosity. She says the recommendations are an 'adult-orientated solution in which the adult world decides how much it is good for children to know about their

The government view, therefore, is that children born following donation should have a right to information which will be prescribed in regulations. This would follow on from a legal right of all adults over 18 to find out whether they were born following gamete or embryo donation. This right would necessitate the establishment of a register of information by the Statutory Licensing Authority (SLA), and would not be retroactive. The tone of the white paper suggests that the available information would be very limited and no indication is given at this stage about the spirit in which it is felt this right should be promoted and facilitated. There would, however, be considerable practical difficulties in maintaining a comprehensive register of information. Treatment centres will only hold information about successful treatment leading to pregnancy. Maternity units will not know at delivery how a baby was conceived. Thus the register will rely substantially on information from parents, yet there is already research evidence to suggest that the vast majority have no intention of telling the child, let alone the SLA.

The Warnock Report recommended that, as with DI, parents of a child born as a result of embryo donation should be entitled to add 'by donation' in the birth register. This followed a recognition of 'principles of good practice' including 'openness with a child about his [or her] genetic origins'. Acceptance of similar principles presumably led the government to express the view that: 'Treatment centres would be *required* [our emphasis] to explain to potential parents the importance of providing this information in the interests of the child' and that couples should be 'strongly encouraged to tell the treatment centre or SLA of any resulting birth.' Such sentiments imply a real recognition of the issue. However, not only the available research on donation, but also major and substantial work on adoption, indicate the extreme difficulties experienced by parents in telling their children the truth about their origins. To deal appropriately with a subject felt by many to be so threatening and painful requires maturity, personal security and sensitivity of a high order. Parents will not be helped to deal with it simply by explanation or encouragement. This approach contains echoes of early adoption practice when many adopters stated their intention, no doubt honestly meant, to 'tell' the child but, as we have seen, few really dealt with this in a meaningful fashion for the child.

Our own and other research suggests that only those parents who have really come to terms with their own infertility, who can fully and honestly accept that donation or indeed adoption are entirely bona fide methods of establishing a family, can begin to deal adequately with 'telling'. Even then they need to accept that 'telling' is not enough but that biographical information is the 'bricks and mortar' of identity development, and they need to feel strong enough in the relationship not to be threatened by the presence of the 'hidden parent'. Secrecy will almost certainly cast a shadow and create a tension in the family which is likely to be detrimental to all.

It would seem clear from research and experience that in such difficult circumstances parents not only need very skilled help to address these issues but also, as in adoption, need a degree of formal reinforcement of the rights of the child. The government has, however, firmly supported the paramountcy of the rights of *parents* in this issue and concluded that any attempt to impose a requirement on parents to report births following donation would 'constitute an unacceptable intrusion on the privacy of couples'.

The existence of large numbers of children already born as a result of donation is not addressed by the white paper. Neither is the Warnock recommendation that the SLA should 'be asked to consider the need for follow-up studies of children born as a result of new techniques'. This was argued from the concern that 'only through such studies would it be possible to assess the long-term consequences, both physical, psychological and developmental of the use of these techniques.'

There are some further indications of concern for the child in Warnock, though again they are not combined into one body of issues nor are they translated into forceful recommendations. The explanation for this could lie in a later comment by Lady Warnock about the committee: 'The only way such a committee can produce the appearance of consensus out of pluralism is to give with one hand and take away with the other; to put one point of view and then immediately weigh against it another, until the issue is irrevocably fudged.' However, the report makes sufficient statements about the importance of honesty and openness and about the need for follow-up studies to lend weight to the view that the white paper is equivocal on

113

its stance regarding access to information.

In stating the intention to keep the situation under review no information is offered concerning what, or whose, 'attitudes' might change and there is no debate in Warnock or the white paper about whether these attitudes are justifiable in the context of present knowledge or research evidence. Even more worrying is the absence of any indication of how the position will be reviewed, what information will be monitored in this process or what tests should be applied in deciding to grant access to identifying information at a later stage.

Retroactive legislation will bring its own problems, and it can be argued that there is now available relevant knowledge, evidence and practical experience upon which to base an informed and thorough debate of the issues. Given that DI has been practised for at least 50 years, and embryo transplant and donation for about ten, such a debate is hardly premature. Refusal to generate full and balanced consideration of the human dignity, rights and needs of the subjects of these procedures would seem insupportable in a sophisticated and civilised society. This is particularly so when the individuals concerned have no lobby or pressure group to press what might be their case.

Chapters 2, 3 and 4 have explored in some detail the fact that the growing-up tasks of achieving a mature independence, a clear sense of identity, and of being able to give and receive love are inextricably linked with knowledge and feelings about heritage. These chapters also sought to illustrate from research that simply being honest is not enough and that even where adopters have been open and honest with their children about the fact of their adoption, a vacuum is experienced at an important point in development. The parallels here between the problems of adopted young people and those born following donation seem very similar and surely practice in one area could very helpfully be informed by experience and research in the other.

These chapters also explored the concept of stigma as developed and described by Goffman.[17] Again there are parallels with adoption and the context of feelings about infertility produces similar strategies of 'control of information' and 'secrecy and collusion'. As Goffman says, these strategies may help individuals to operate more or less effectively in social situations but they do not eliminate the feelings which give rise to the strategies. Warnock and the white paper acknowledge this desire for secrecy in various ways without addressing the potent sources of this desire or analysing the potential for good or ill. We know from many adult adopted people that secrets arising from a lurking doubt in adoptive parents about the validity and acceptability of their parenthood, can be a source of great tension and a destructive force in a family. The potential for similar problems in families resulting from donation would seem to be as great, for similar reasons.

It has to be acknowledged here too that any 'solution' does not simply lie in the hands of the family and those professionals who may be offering therapeutic help. There must be a collective responsibility to rethink the philosophical, sociological and psychological bases of families established by other than 'natural' means, for general attitudes to infertility and childlessness have much to do with the development of feelings of stigma. If such families were seen as different but as valid and acceptable as 'natural' families, the need for secrecy would disappear. Perhaps this is a naive hope, but collective collusion in promoting continuing secrecy would not seem to serve the long-term interests of either child or parent.

Fitness for parenthood
In Chapter 2 of the Warnock Report reference was made to evidence which expressed concern that infertility treatment could be provided without 'due regard for the interests of any child that may be born as a result'. The possibility of Schedule 1 offenders* seeking treatment was cited. Other evidence argued that the interests of the child require that he or she should be born into a loving, stable, heterosexual relationship. Reference has already been made earlier in this chapter to the claims that infertility treatment is a right founded in the European Convention on Human Rights. This argument was extended to include homosexual relationships and single parents, the latter group being further supported by comparisons with adoption legislation which specifically provides for single parents. The committee was broadly of the view that children should be born into a two-parent heterosexual family thus accepting in principle some element of selection. The view was also expressed by the committee that there may be valid reasons why infertility treatment should not be offered as it might be deemed

---

*Schedule 1 of the 1933 Children and Young Persons Act lists offences against children. A person shall not be approved as a foster parent if convicted of any of these offences.

115

to be 'not in the best interests of the patient, the child . . . or the patient's immediate family'. In subsequent comment, however, the committee appears to have withdrawn from the issue, declining to recommend an objective selection process, and leaving the matter in the hands of the consultant who, it is implied, will consult with health and social work colleagues and make a decision. There is a firm recommendation that a decision not to treat should be explained to the patient in full. The report recognises in its own words that the decisions will involve 'social judgements that go beyond the purely medical', and the committee even considered whether to try and draw up 'social criteria' but decided that 'it was not possible to draw up comprehensive criteria that would be sensitive to the circumstances of every case'. The report therefore seems to recognise that some form of screening might be necessary, but does not express reservations about the fact that the selection and training of medical practitioners does not equip them for this task. Nor does it question that the main focus of the medical practitioner, that of achieving successful treatment, might cloud or compromise the selection issues. It seems to imply an informal multi-disciplinary process of consultation leading to the selection decision, but does not contemplate the pitfalls inherent in informal subjective processes which may need to be justified in retrospect. Nor does it consider the basis upon which potential parents might engage in this process, or choose to question it, or the basis upon which other agencies such as the police might be asked to provide essential information; for how else would significant facts, such as a history of violence or child molestation, be established, unless by hearsay?

In our view compelling evidence on this point argued that 'the greater the degree of intervention in the creation of a child, the more responsibility must be taken for that child'. The Warnock Committee seemed to some extent to be influenced by this view but then left the issue in limbo, creating a scenario which does not in any way acknowledge highly relevant adoption experience in this area. There is much potential in the situation described for practices to develop which will carry similar problems to the third-party adoption placements (now outlawed) made by medical practitioners and nurses in the past. The termination of this practice was based upon the developing knowledge that the selection and preparation of people to become nurturing, rather than biological, parents required specific skills and experience.

The white paper too was equivocal on this issue. It notes the differing views on formal assessment, but comments at greater length upon the arguments against selection. These are, briefly, that 'there was no assessment of couples who conceived naturally', that those who had faced problems of infertility had 'often thought through their attitudes to parenthood more deeply than those able to conceive without difficulty' and that the children were 'very much wanted'. There is no indication in those statements of any recognition of the profound differences between natural conception and the responsibilities inherent in positive intervention designed to help to produce a child. Further, vague generalisations about wanted children and attitudes having been thought through more deeply may not be felt to be worthy of a serious document which will be the basis of legislation.

The white paper therefore concludes that a formal statutory procedure to assess suitability would not be appropriate. It appears to concede the point immediately however, if rather ambiguously, in the next sentence which states that: 'In considering whether to grant a licence the SLA will be required to take account of centres' procedures for deciding whether to offer treatment to particular couples.' There is no clue to government thinking on what guidance will be given to the SLA and to centres in developing and assessing these procedures.

References

1 Report of the Committee of Inquiry into human fertilisation and embryology (Warnock Report) (Cmnd 9314) HMSO, 1984.

2 Warnock M *A question of life* Basil Blackwell, 1985.

3 Human fertilisation and embryology: a framework for legislation (Cmnd 259) HMSO, 1987.

4 Trend M 'Misconceived experiments' *Spectator*, 16 January 1988.

5 In the *Guardian*, 25 July 1988; where it was also reported that Mrs Gena Dodd of 'Triangle' claimed that '100 surrogate babies have been born in Britain since 1980 and many more are planned'.

6 Snowden R, Mitchell G D and Snowden E M *Artificial reproduction: a social investigation* Allen and Unwin, 1983.

7 Houghton D and Houghton P *Coping with childlessness* Allen and Unwin, 1984.

8 Snowden R and Snowden E *The gift of a child* Allen and Unwin, 1984.

9 National Association for the Childless, 318 Summers Lane, Birmingham B19 3RG.

10 Hull M G R et al 'Population study of causes, treatment and outcome of infertility' *British Medical Journal* 291, 1985.

11 Chargaff E 'Engineering a molecular nightmare' *Nature* 327 6119, 1987.

12 Legislation on human infertility services and embryo research (Cmnd 46) HMSO, 1986.

13 Phillips M 'Expert guide wanted for the gene map' *Guardian* 12 December 1988.

14 See 2 above.

15 McWhinnie A 'AID and infertility' *Adoption & fostering* 10 1, 1986.

16 Mitchell G D 'The family and society' in *AID and after* BAAF, 1984.

17 Goffman E *Stigma: notes on the management of spoiled identity* Penguin Books, 1963.

6 Issues for further consideration

Previous chapters have been about identity, human rights, stigma, psychological continuity, concepts of family and parenting and attitudes to infertility, childlessness and the formation of families through non 'natural' means.

The summary of our small research project and the follow-up discussion group with adopted adults has been set against a historical background and in the context of other research and writing since the introduction of adoption in 1926. Implications for present and future practice have been suggested. The background and context to current discussions about human fertilisation have been described and some parallels with adoption experience drawn. In the process of considering these questions some important themes have emerged. In conclusion, therefore, we want briefly to highlight those themes as a contribution to the discussion within the social work profession and the wider public and parliamentary context. These are:–
– a recognition of the analogy between key aspects of adoption and human fertilisation programmes, and an acceptance of the relevance of adoption research and experience
– the role of social work
– attitudes to children and their rights
– the need for research.

Analogies with adoption
It is eminently understandable that 'telling' poses many difficult and emotive questions for adoptive parents. It is also clear from at least one research study that parents of children born of DI have similar problems.[1] In fact it is suggested that the vast majority of parents have not told, and do not intend to tell, their children the truth. One commentator has gone so far as to say 'the average AID child who has not been told about the AID will be as certain of its origins as any other child. The fact that it is mistaken about the origin of half its genes is to my mind of no importance whatsoever.'[2] Yet in our research project,

and confirmed elsewhere, the ability of adoptive parents to deal openly and honestly with the adopted child in all matters *particularly those relating to origins* was seen as their single most important attribute. What possible reason can there be for suggesting that children born as a result of DI or embryology should feel significantly differently? How much to tell, when, and the availability of accurate information are basic and difficult questions. Whether the telling will 'unsettle' the child or even cause him or her to love the nurturing parent less is hard to face and often avoided.

The implications for dealing fully and sensitively with such matters for potential parents are particularly difficult. How can they contemplate aspects of the healthy development of the child they do not yet have? How do social workers and others make this a real issue for potential parents in an unreal situation? At least in the adoption situation there is a generally stated acceptance that the notion of telling children about their origins is 'a good thing' and this is reinforced by the legal rights of young people to certain information about their origins after the age of 18. As we have seen, at the present time there is not even a general acceptance that children born of donation could and should be told the truth about their origins. We have also seen, however, that people have a need and a right to know about their biological heritage – overwhelmingly through adoption research, but also argued persuasively in relation to DI, notably by McWhinnie.[3]

The white paper on human fertilisation and embryology is firm in its recommendations about a counselling service. This covers factual information about the medical procedures and options available and the potential stresses of treatment. Counselling is also to be provided where treatment using donated material is considered and should focus on the implications for the future family of 'having a child which is not genetically theirs'. The white paper also recommends counselling for donors, to explain the implications of donation and the legal framework. It is clear that the government considers counselling to be an important element in the provision of infertility services and that this should be carried out by someone with appropriate qualifications: indeed, the quality of these services will be taken into consideration by the SLA when granting a licence to a centre. Obviously this will have implications for the composition of the SLA. Legislation has already placed social work firmly in the business of finding permanent substitute families for children deprived of their own families and of counselling all individuals with problems relating to adoption. The emphasis and priority derives quite properly from the notion that adoption is essentially a service for children. In this fundamental respect adoption is obviously different from fertilisation and donation procedures. However, most of the other important issues in adoptive families and families facilitated by donation are essentially similar both for parents and for children. Clearly social work has the skills and the potential to provide and develop a counselling service. However, it should be presented in such a way that it does not demean the recipient: as already related, many of our research respondents felt diminished by the surroundings in which their interviews took place and by the impression that their problems were a low priority in comparison to other demands on social work time.

This is perhaps an opportune time for serious consideration of the provision of a comprehensive social work service in the fields of infertility, childlessness, fertilisation treatments and adoption – either as an independent service or provided as a specialist division of local authority social services departments. The basis for the second model is already in place and would seem to be preferable. Specialist fostering and adoption sections already exist in most departments, and there is also a well-established and effective model of local authority social workers within clinical teams in other specialisms, including infertility. Thus the foundation for a service is already in place, with expertise relevant to fertility programmes. This service should at least inform but preferably have representation on the SLA.

Meticulous records would of course have to be kept and parents and children encouraged and helped to refer back at times when therapeutic help from an external source may be necessary. This would be a practical recognition that to be a nurturing parent but not a biological parent, or to have two parents one of whom might be a biological and one not, presents many different considerations and potential problems in the parenting and growing-up processes. It would also recognise the near impossibility of giving real and lasting help to potential parents on these issues before the child is even a reality. To legitimate needs and rights in such an open and acceptable manner would, we feel, be a very desirable development.

In our view this debate must encompass the question of selection for treatment. As has been demonstrated, both the Warnock Report and the white paper seem to concede that some element of selection already takes place. They go further to the extent of accepting that in some way selection should be enshrined in the procedures of the 'centres' and considered by the SLA. This very important question is, however, then left in a vague and dangerous vacuum which seems to suggest that doctors will make the selection on the basis of some sort of consultation with some other disciplines. There has been no dicussion of what criteria would be seen as important. Claims about rights to infertility treatment deriving from interpretations of the United Nations and European Conventions on human rights must surely be contested. It would seem naive, and even dishonest, for potential parents and practitioners to see this purely in terms of rights to treatment. As McWhinnie has said: 'in reality they [practitioners] are providing a service which artificially create families. They are so patient-oriented and wanting the best for their patients that they are giving only cursory thought to the long-term welfare and interest of the children thus created. They, too, have rights and needs and should not be used instrumentally in this way solely to fulfill the wishes and needs of adults. Simply to desire a child does not automatically make you even potentially a good parent.'[4]

We would urge strongly that especially where donation is involved a formal selection procedure should be introduced which explictly recognises the responsibilities to children inherent in the direct intervention to create families. In this context, it has to be said that much expertise already exists in the adoption field in the selection of parents.

An immediate obstacle to be overcome in providing a properly-founded service of the kind described is the current very limited acceptance of the issues and problems surrounding families developed through donation. There are very clear echoes in the white paper of the secrecy and the primacy of the rights of adults which permeated thinking in the early stages of adoption. Yet we have seen through ample evidence that access to full information is handled in an overwhelmingly sensitive and appropriate way by adopted people. This was the experience too of the Scottish system which was in place 20 years before legislation was introduced in England and Wales. The fears of disaster, blackmail and the destruction of other people's lives such as were predicted by some leading politicians and media pundits in the debates about access to adoption records have proved groundless. It must be the fervent hope that this hard evidence, rather than the subjective and emotional discussion on access to information for adoptive people will inform the debate on the bill now before Parliament.

The principle of right to information about genetic origins is now established as inalienable in adoption practice. It therefore seems illogical that in the case of children born as a result of donation and human fertilisation procedures the government proposes that the right of a child to information is to be proscribed. The protection of the donor's anonymity, and the possibility of donors being deterred by the prospect of more information being made available, is, as the white paper itself acknowledges, refuted by Swedish experience. The 'protection' of the prospective parents, as has already been discussed, is questionable from a number of standpoints, including that of the interests of the prospective parents themselves.

Social work

As a corollary to the suggested development of a comprehensive social work service, some reflection on the public face of social work would seem to be warranted. Our research indicated that, once engaged with social workers, respondents immediately appreciated the benefits and recognised the skills exercised. They nevertheless had considerable difficulty in overcoming stereotypes about social work and social services. As a profession, we are perhaps our own worst enemies in failing to rebut some of the more inaccurate and insulting popular portrayals of social work. We also fail to promote a positive and accurate image of the breadth, depth and variety of the skills and services offered to people of all social classes. Denial of skills, paraded as 'anti-elitism', has not helped. In the eyes of many, social work appears to be completely identified with political causes and the more financial- and materially-deprived social classes. However, the high incidence in the community of physical and mental illness and of disability, serious injury and accident, as well as the high number of casualties of broken marriages, bereavement, unemployment and broken family relationships, demonstrates that misfortune and impaired functioning of all kinds is no respecter of persons. In all these, and in many other situations, social workers have a valuable and important part to play in helping those affected to resolve their difficulties and return to healthy and effective social functioning.

Social work therefore needs to accept that it currently faces almost a crisis of credibility and certainly a low public image. In small ways this is apparent in the use of words like 'counselling' which increasingly seems to portray the 'respectable' side of social work. As Louis Blom Cooper suggested in 1988,[5] social work needs to 'grow up' in the professional sense of being clear about the maintenance of standards and ethics, professional training and the defence of itself and its members. It has, in other words, to be seen to put its house in order. This must include most careful attention, in the interests of clients, to the environment within which social work is conducted and the image and attitudes it portrays.

The rights of children

It seems to the authors that there is a socio-political tradition in this country in which battles about children's rights, needs and status are hard won and are almost always followed by a reaction.

Facing the possibility that British society may not really be child-respecting is uncomfortable. Of course the vast majority of British families love and cherish their children very much indeed. Some of the institutions and practices within society, however, do give cause for concern – for example our attitude towards corporal punishment has differed markedly from most other European countries and we continue to incarcerate a higher number of children and young people than they do, as part of our provision for juvenile justice. Lord Justice Butler Sloss[6] drew attention to the need to see the child 'as a person' but preoccupations with the interests and position of adults, rather than children, generally seem to dominate considerations which involve both. The traditional view that children were the possessions of their parents and that the interests of both coincide still seems to be prevalent in many sectors of society. It could be said that the statement in the 1975 Children Act clarifying the position regarding the relative importance of and difference between children's interests and parents' interests was, and still is, ahead of its time.[7] Interestingly, the recent Department of Health guidelines for staff working in the child sexual abuse area[8] illustrates some ambivalence and re-introduces a perspective which seems to shift the emphasis back towards parents' rights. For example, whilst the section on the content of training in the guidelines states that emphasis should be placed on the interests of the child, there are several other inferences which seem to introduce an equality of concern for the rights of parents and children in what is, by definition, a very unequal situation. The guidelines appear to stress that 'staff should allow for the possibility of other explanations' rather than a wholehearted belief in what children tell us.

By implication, the white paper and the bill on human fertilisation continue to deny the rights of children and young people born as a result of donation. While this seems illogical in the face of rights of others in similar circumstances and of available relevant knowledge, it is perhaps more understandable in the context of the underlying trend suggested above.

The need for research
Reference was made in our introduction and in the last chapter to the possibility contemplated in the white paper of changes in attitude and of retrospective legislation. The fear, anxiety and anger this will provoke for donors and parents who have entered into a contract in good faith are entirely predictable. A cynical view might be that this paragraph (84) in the white paper is no more than tokenism, as retrospective legislation will become much too difficult to contemplate. It seems unlikely that there will be any significant developments in the foreseeable future to enhance the state of knowledge which already exists; it is tempting therefore to conclude that this is simply a prevaricating measure born of an unwillingness to face up to the issue now. If retrospective legislation is considered it seems entirely predictable that there will be a re-run of the, at times, almost hysterical debate about the adoption legislation which gave rise to access to birth records.

Our argument would of course be that legislation should immediately address and introduce the measures we have discussed, particularly bringing the right to information in line with the rights of adopted people. At the very least, however, we believe that research should be commissioned to gather and analyse information on the experiences of people who have grown up in families where one or both nurturing parents were different from the biological parents. Criteria should also be established by which, at a later stage, proper reviews may take place: this will be facilitated by the establishment of a register as recommended in the white paper. Again, it must be argued that if review and the possibility of retrospective legislation are to be taken seriously there must be very careful regulation by the Statutory

Licensing Authority to ensure that fuller records are kept than may be required by the initial legislation.

The thrust of our argument has inevitably been a concern to counterbalance prevailing attitudes. This does not, however, imply any lack of sympathy with the position of childless couples anxious, indeed desperate, to have children. Ideally such people should be free from unwanted pressures and assumptions on the part of others and we would wish to see a well-orchestrated and executed attempt to achieve more sympathetic and better-informed public attitudes. Sadly, however, not all human problems are capable of resolution, and caution must especially be exercised when there is a danger that what appears to be a short-term 'solution' contains the seeds of long-term problems. In the enthusiasm and excitement which surrounds scientific breakthrough there is an understandable tendency to underestimate inherent difficulties. The developmental problems which, however unwittingly, may be created for persons yet unborn may be profound. By dint of personal experience or professional practice only a minority of the population has considered the underlying issues, and herein lies one of the difficulties in generating proper debate about the coming legislation.

Doctors, lawyers, social workers, moral philosophers, adopted people, childless people and potential donors all have a major contribution to make to the consideration of these issues. In the interest of present and future generations of children the white paper should not be allowed to pass into legislation without this discussion.

Failure to address these issues will, we believe, reinforce a serious limitation of fundamental human rights as well as impoverished helping responses to childless people and to people born as a result of direct medical intervention. The 'dark secret' referred to by one of the respondents in our research will continue to exert its damaging influence, clouding the lives of a significant number of people.

References

1 Snowden R, Mitchell G D and Snowden E M *Artificial reproduction: a social investigation* Allen and Unwin, 1983.

2 Joyce D N 'The implications of greater openness concerning AID' in *AID and after* BAAF, 1984.

3 McWhinnie A 'AID and infertility' *Adoption & fostering* 10 1, 1986.

4 See 3 above.

5 Blom-Cooper L *Social Work Today* 31 March 1988.

6 Report of the Inquiry into child abuse in Cleveland (The Butler-Sloss Report) (Cmnd 412) HMSO, 1987.

7 Child Care Act 1980, section 18 (formerly Children Act 1975.)

8 *Working with child sexual abuse: guidelines for training social services staff* Department of Health 1989.

British Agencies for Adoption & Fostering

British Agencies for Adoption & Fostering (BAAF) is a registered charity and professional association for all those working in the child care field. BAAF's work includes:

providing training and consultation services to social workers and other professionals to help them improve the quality of medical, legal and social work services to children and families;

giving evidence to government committees on subjects concerning children and families;

responding to consultative documents on changes in legislation and regulations affecting children in or at risk of coming into care;

publishing a wide range of books, training packs and leaflets as well as a quarterly journal on adoption, fostering and child care issues;

giving advice and information to members of the public on aspects of adoption, fostering and child care issues;

and helping to find new families for children through the BAAF Exchange Service, 'Be My Parent' and 'Find a Family'.

More information about BAAF (including membership subscription details) can be obtained from BAAF, 11 Southwark Street, London SE1 1RQ.